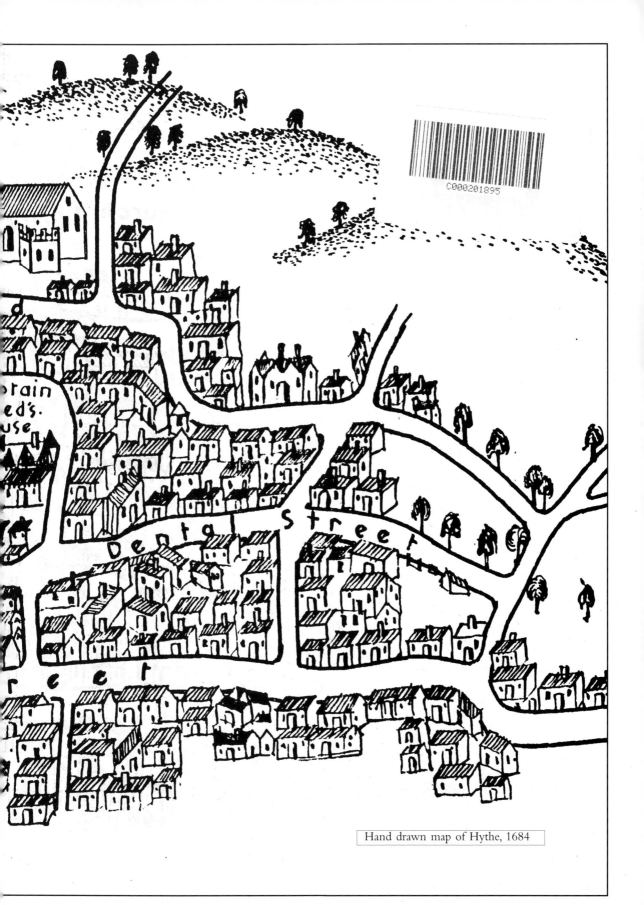

C000201895

Hand drawn map of Hythe, 1684

HYTHE
A HISTORY

The First World War tank pictured in the High Street upon its presentation to the town on 11 July 1919.

HYTHE
A HISTORY

Martin Easdown
& Linda Sage

Phillimore

2004

Published by
PHILLIMORE & CO. LTD
Shopwyke Manor Barn, Chichester, West Sussex, England

© Martin Easdown and Linda Sage, 2004

ISBN 1 86077 315 X

Printed and bound in Great Britain by
THE CROMWELL PRESS
Trowbridge, Wiltshire

For Tom and Bethany

Contents

❧

List of Illustrations

❧❧❧

Frontispiece: Tank in Hythe High Street

Acknowledgements

We would sincerely like to thank all the people who have assisted us in the preparation of this book and provided us with information and illustrations. Our particular thanks go to Peter and Annie Bamford who generously allowed us to use their research and information on Seabrook. Peter Hooper and Alan F. Taylor were most kind in allowing us to copy postcards from their excellent collections. Barbara Clarke, Rachel Watts, Miss F.D.L. Laundon, George Newman, Pam and Michael Dray and Eamonn Rooney helpfully provided information on Hythe. We would also like to thank the staff at Hythe Library and the East Kent Archive Centre for their patience and kindness.

Illustration Acknowledgements

Peter and Annie Bamford, 42-3, 47, 55, 60, 78-9, 97, 107, 119, 131-2, 134-5; Peter Hooper, 20, 24, 71, 76, 89, 96, 98, 106, 118, 124; Alan F. Taylor, 41, 75, 83, 91, 125; Rachel Watts, 2. All other illustrations are from the authors' Marlinova Collection.

I

Home to the Invader

As befits one of the historic Cinque Ports, the name of Hythe is taken from the Saxon word for a haven or landing place. The origins of the town, however, lie in the Roman settlement of *Portus Lemanis* (present-day Lympne), some two miles north-west of modern Hythe.

The Romans first landed at nearby Deal in 55 and 54 B.C., but their stay proved short-lived and they did not return until A.D.43 when the Emperor Claudius ordered his general Aulus Plautius to invade Britain. *Rutupiae* (Richborough) was established as their chief port and *Durovernum* (Canterbury) as their army headquarters. A system of straight roads in the Roman tradition connected the two, and also *Durovernum* to *Requlbium* (Reculver), *Dubris* (Dover), *Durobrivae* (Rochester) and *Portus Lemanis* (Lympne), the road to the latter being known as Stone Street.

Vessels from *Portus Lemanis* usually sailed to *Gesoriacum* (Boulogne), and to defend the English Channel the Romans formed a British fleet, the *Classis Britannica*, placed under the command of *Comes Litoris Saxonici*, the Count of the Saxon Shore. However, from the third century A.D. the fleet was unable to prevent increasing attacks by Saxon tribes, and fortresses were erected at their ports including Stutfall Castle, built in 280 to defend the harbour of

Portus Lemanis at West Hythe, which was then the mouth of the River Rother (Limen).

The word 'Stutfall' was taken from the Saxon for strong fortress '*Stout Wale*' and the remains can still be viewed below Lympne Castle. In 1850 Stutfall was excavated by Roach Smith who discovered it was originally a seven-sided building that covered an area of ten acres, with steps leading down to the harbour. The walls were 20-25 feet in height and 12-14 feet thick with an imposing towered gateway on the eastern wall. From an early date, land subsidence caused by underground streams damaged the castle and a quantity of its stone was used in the construction of Lympne Castle and church on the promontory above.

The somnolent great stone walls still cling precariously to what was once the cliff of the Roman seashore, just as H.G. Wells described them in *Kipps* in 1905: 'You look down the sheep-dotted slopes to where, beside the canal and under the trees, the crumbled memories of Rome sleep for ever.'

From the fallen masonry of Stutfall Castle can be seen a range of hills that stretches away to the south-west: this was the old coastline of the Roman era. All the land that presently lies between the hills and the sea, comprising principally Romney Marsh, was reclaimed behind a sand and shingle bank formed by

1. The Roman Stutfall Castle, as drawn by George Shepherd in 1829.

the continuous wave action of the sea. The build-up of shingle blocked the mouth of the Rother Estuary at West Hythe to such an extent that the western end became unusable and the river was diverted to Romney. The Romans erected the Rhee Wall, a large channel with an embankment on each side, to carry the waters of the river from Romney to Appledore.

By 430 *Portus Lemanis* had been left high and dry and the Romans had fled Britain in the face of mounting raids by Saxons, Picts and Scots, to defend their homeland from attacks by Goths. The native Britons were left to look after themselves and assistance was sought by their king, Vortigern, from the Jutish chiefs Hengist and Horsa, who landed at Ebbsfleet, north of Richborough, in 449. The Picts were driven off and as a reward Hengist (Horsa having

been killed) was invested with the government of Kent. However, this led to more Jutes and Saxons crossing the Channel and fighting broke out with the Britons, including an encounter that was said to have taken place between Folkestone and Hythe. The Britons were driven from Kent following bloody battles at Aylesford and Crayford and Hengist was proclaimed King of Kent.

Following the decline of *Portus Lemanis*, West Hythe hung on as a small port, in spite of the constant threat of its harbour silting up. In 732 King Ethelbert of Kent made a grant of land there to Queen Ethelburga's Convent, Lyminge. The land, at Sandtun, was situated close to the Saxon harbour. 'A Chapel of our Lady' was established there in Norman times, but by this time West Hythe, a Cinque Port limb of Hythe,

2. The remains of West Hythe Church in 1829, drawn by George Shepherd. On the hill above, Lympne Castle and church can just be seen.

was being abandoned by the sea and eventually dwindled away to just a few settlements. The roof of the chapel was burnt out in 1620 and subsequently became a ruin, and in 1840 the parish was united with Lympne.

Botolph's Bridge, which crosses the Royal Military Canal at West Hythe, and the nearby inn of the same name, both commemorate the legend that the body of St Botolph was hidden there from the Danes. The inn sign features a shaft of light that was said to have shone down from the dark night sky to assist the monks in carrying the coffin across what was then a creek.

During the decline of West Hythe in the ninth and tenth centuries, the new port of Hythe was established at the navigable eastern end of the old estuary. In 853 it was the scene of a great battle between King Ethelwulf of England and a large Danish army, during which a great many men perished. By 1052 the harbour was well established and received an unwelcome visit from the powerful Earl Godwin and his sons (including the future King Harold II) who burnt ships in the harbour and put inhabitants to the sword. Nevertheless, Hythe was about to enter the greatest period of its history as one of the new Cinque Ports.

2
Cinque Port High

The Cinque Ports confederation was formed to supply ship service to King Edward the Confessor (1042-66) and consisted of the five main ports of Dover, Hastings, Sandwich, Romney and Hythe, along with corporate and non-corporate members known as limbs. Dover, as the head port at the time, was liable to supply 20 ships for 15 days each year: Sandwich and Romney were also known to have owed ship service and so probably did Hastings and Hythe. In return for providing a fleet to defend the vulnerable Channel coast, the five ports were granted various privileges, including the right to hold a court of law, freedom from various taxes and 'Honours at Court' – the right of the Cinque Port representatives to carry the canopy over a monarch at a coronation. The Cinque Port barons now line the west side of the screen in Westminster Abbey and receive the two standards carried before the sovereign. One other privilege, known as 'Den and Strond', granted the portsmen rights to sell herring and mend nets at Yarmouth, which led to considerable friction with the Norfolk port. By 1190 the 'Two Ancient Towns' of Rye and Winchelsea had been added to the confederation.

In 1066 the Cinque Ports fleet sailed northwards to assist King Harold in repelling an invasion by his brother Tostig and Harald Hardrada of Norway. However, this left only a few ships in the English Channel on watch to resist the attack of William of Normandy. A few of the Romney contingent did manage to cause some casualties among the Normans, which led William to 'take such vengeance as he would for the slaughter of his men'. Notwithstanding, William recognised the value of the Ports and confirmed the charters of Edward the Confessor, as did all of his successors, with the exception of the troubled King Stephen during his reign of the 'Nineteen Long Winters' (1135-54).

At the time of Domesday Book in 1086, Hythe was a Bailiwick in the Manor of Saltwood, despite having a larger population (of 225 families) than its village neighbour and, until 1100, its own mint. The book records the manor:

> was taxed at 7 sulings [a suling was 160 acres] in the time of Edward the Confessor, and now for three sulings; land for 15 ploughs. In lordship there are 2 ploughs and 33 villagers, with 12 smallholders having 9½ ploughs. There is a church and 2 slaves, and 9 mills at 20 shillings, and 33 acres of meadow, wood sufficient for the pannage of 80 pigs. To this manor belong 225 burgesses in the Borough of Hede [Hythe]. Between the borough and the manor, in the time of Edward the Confessor it was worth £16, when he received it £8, now in the whole £29 6s.4d.

3. The decayed grandeur of Saltwood Castle, viewed by two gentlemen in the 1880s.

Hythe's bailiff was appointed by the Archbishop of Canterbury, who held the manor, although occasionally the barons of Hythe were allowed to choose their own bailiffs and jurats.

The Manor of Saltwood was controlled from Saltwood Castle, said to date back to 488 when Aesc, son of Hengist, built the first castle. The earliest documentary evidence occurs in 1026 when Earl Haldene granted the Manor of 'Saltwuude' to the monks of Christ Church, Canterbury. Edward the Confessor confirmed the grant and the manor passed to the most powerful man in the kingdom, Earl Godwin.

Following the Norman Conquest, William I bestowed Saltwood upon Archbishop Lanfranc and in Domesday Book it is recorded as being held by Hugo de Montfort, by Knight's Service. During the reign of Henry II (1154-89) the castle came into the hands of Henry d'Essex, Lord Warden of the Cinque Ports, who had it rebuilt. However, in 1163 he was accused of cowardice and treason by Robert de Montfort in battle against the Welsh and was challenged by him to a duel. Essex, who was the older man, lost and was left for dead. Fortunately a group of monks found him still to be alive and nursed him back to health. With all his wealth and estates gone, the humiliated earl decided to stay with the monks for the remainder of his life.

4.   The ruinous dungeon of Saltwood Castle pictured in the 1870s.

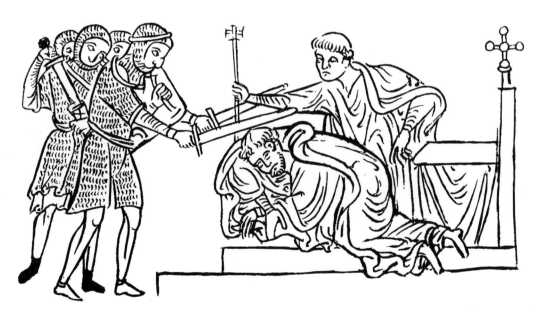

5.   The murder of Thomas Becket in Canterbury Cathedral on 29 December 1170, as depicted in a drawing by Matthew Paris in around 1240.

King Henry seized the castle and appointed Ranulf de Broc, who held the nearby Brockhill Estate, as its castellan. De Broc was a particularly fierce opponent of the Archbishop of Canterbury, Thomas Becket, who was in exile from 1164-70. Becket's exile followed a disagreement with the King over the boundaries of influence of the Church and its rights to try clergy in its own courts. Ranulf showed what he thought of Becket by seizing (with the assistance of his cousin Robert de Broc) a cargo of the archbishop's wine, and also hunting his deer. This led him to suffer excommunication (which he ignored) in company with the Archbishop of York and the Bishops of London and Salisbury, who during Becket's absence had crowned Henry's eldest son as King Regent in Westminster Abbey on 14 June 1170.

Becket returned to England on 2 December 1170, but incurred the wrath of the King after the excommunicated bishops reached Henry at Bur Castle, near Bayeux in Normandy and informed him what had happened. The King uttered his famous quote, 'Who will rid me of this turbulent priest?' on Christmas Day 1170 and four knights – Reginald FitzUrse, Hugh de Moreville, William de Tracy and Richard le Breton – took him at his word and dashed across the Channel. They were entertained for the night by Ranulf de Broc at Saltwood Castle, which it was said he had turned into a 'den of thieves', and on the following morning, 29 December 1170, Robert de Broc accompanied them along Stone Street and into Canterbury. The four knights made their way into the cathedral and, having found Becket, FitzUrse struck him a glancing blow. Another followed from de Tracy before a slash from le Breton finished Becket off by severing his upper skull.

During the reign of Henry's son John (1199-1216) the castle was restored to the Church and became a regular residence for archbishops. Following damage by an earthquake in 1380 (which allowed William Thorpe, who had been imprisoned in the north tower for 16 years, to make his escape), Archbishop William Courtenay enlarged the keep and staterooms were added. An impressive gateway was erected by architect Henry Yevele, modelled on his Westgate in Canterbury.

Saltwood's parish church of St Peter and St Paul was once the mother church to the parish church of Hythe, St Leonard's, and they were not formally separated until 1844. The chancel and nave of the building date from 1150, with the tower being added around 1220. The church is noted for its monumental brasses, particularly the head and shoulders brass of 1370 commemorating Johannes Verien. A fine east window was added in 1330.

Lympne Castle, boasting a wonderful panoramic view across Romney Marsh, was also once held by Christ Church, Canterbury and Becket was known to have resided there as archdeacon. Built on the site of a Roman lookout, the Saxon abbey was rebuilt in Norman times as a fortified residence for the archbishopric using stone from the ruinous Stutfall Castle below on the cliff. The work on the castle, along with the adjoining church, was carried out by the first Norman Archbishop of Canterbury, Lanfranc, who incorporated the archdeacon's residence into the Saxon abbey's lodging house. In the 12th century a square tower with walls five feet thick was added at the eastern end and during the Second World

6. Lympne Castle in the 1870s, seen from the slope that leads down to Stutfall Castle and the Romney Marsh.

7. Saltwood Church before its Victorian restoration, in a view probably taken in the 1870s or 1880s.

War this was modified for use as a look-out post. The Great Tower at the western end was built in 1360, the rounded section being added around sixty years later. The main feature of the interior was the Great Hall, with its Tudor panelling and large fireplace of 1420.

According to Hasted, the famous 18th-century Kent historian, the church that adjoins Lympne Castle, St Stephen's, was also once part of the archbishopric: 'The church of Limne was part of the ancient possessions of the Archbishopric and continued so till Archbishop Lanfranc gave it to the Archdeaconry, at which time, or very soon afterwards, it seems to have been appropriated to it, being the first possessions it ever had.' The church features a Norman tower of around 1100, which was originally the west tower of a subsequently destroyed Norman nave. The nave, north aisle and chancel were all rebuilt around 1200.

One other castle in the Hythe area is situated at Westenhanger. This is a 14th-century quadrangular castle erected by John de Kiriet in 1344 during a French invasion scare. The north-west tower was named 'Fair Rosamund's Tower' in honour of Rosamund Gifford, a mistress of Henry II who is thought to have stayed at the earlier manor house on the site.

Hythe was at the height of its power as a Cinque Port in the 12th and 13th centuries, which enabled the parish church of St Leonard to be considerably rebuilt between 1156 and 1220. Originally erected in c.1080, St Leonard's was named after the patron saint of prisoners.

8. A postcard of St Stephen's Church, Lympne issued around 1910. The original Norman west tower may be seen in the centre of the church with the later additions surrounding it. Lympne Castle can just be seen on the left.

9.   Fair Rosamund's Tower, Westenhanger Castle in the 1870s.

The north transept, now St Edmund's Chapel, may have incorporated a Saxon place of worship as a Saxon arch can plainly be seen. The church was impressively rebuilt in the fashionable Early English style with a fine choir and sanctuary, and a raised chancel with an ambulatory below. The chancel was subsequently described as having 'the finest chancel of any church in England, not to say Europe' by Professor Francis Bond, a renowned authority on medieval church architecture.

Leland's claim at the time of Henry VIII that an earlier abbey existed on the site of the church cannot be substantiated, although there is evidence of other early churches in Hythe. These include St Michael's, erected halfway between Hythe and West Hythe (the foundations of which can still be discerned in dry weather), and St Nicholas, situated in the current North Road area of Hythe, said to have been in ruins by the early 15th century. Other churches may have existed where bones and skulls have been dug up on Barrack Hill and close to Seabrook Road. A small priory also once existed on Blackhouse Hill during the 12th century. It was attached to St Radigund's Abbey, Dover, but failed to prosper and at one stage the monks were seen wandering about the streets of Hythe begging for food.

In 1278 Edward I confirmed the Cinque Ports' privileges in a general charter, of which Hythe has the only surviving copy, in such

10. A view of St Leonard's Church from the north east taken by the postcard publisher Valentines in about 1910. The unusual 13th-century small D-shaped tower containing the stairway to the triforium and clerestory can be seen.

good condition the Latin script is perfectly legible. Translated into the English, the most important chapter reads:

> Edward by the Grace of God King of England Lord of Ireland and Duke of Aquitaine, to all Archbishops, Bishops, Abbots, Priors, Earls, Barons, Justices, Sheriffs, Reeves, Ministers, and to all Bailiffs, and to his faithful subjects. Greeting. Know ye that for the faithful service that the Barons of our Cinque Ports have aforetime rendered to our ancestors, Kings of England, and latterly to us in our army against Wales, and for their good service to us and our heirs Kings of England faithfully to be continued in time to come, we have granted and by

> this our Charter have confirmed for us and our heirs to the same our Barons and their heirs, all their liberties and freedoms so that they may be quit of all toll, and all customs, to wit, of all lastage [weight duty on goods], tallage [quantity duty on goods], passage [landing tax], cayage, rivage [wharf toll], ponsage [bridge toll], and all wreck [salvage on wrecks without paying tax], and of buying, selling and rebuying throughout our whole land and realm, with soc and sac [paying homage to the king], and thol [freedom from interference] and them [paying homage only to the king], and that they may be wreckfree [others unable to claim salvage on their wrecks], and wittfree [freedom from interference], lastagefree [freedom

11.   The banner of the Cinque Ports as preserved in the council chamber of the Maison Dieu at Dover.

relish. Piracy and the fruits of raiding parties added considerably to the wealth of the ports. In 1292, in co-operation with the Dutch, Irish and Gascon fleets, the Cinque Ports vessels defeated a combined French, Norman, Flemish and Genoese fleet in a pre-arranged battle off the Breton coast. However, the portsmen were not averse to attacking their own side and in 1297, whilst sailing with the royal fleet to fight the French, they suddenly attacked the Yarmouth contingent, sinking 32 ships and killing 200 men.

To complement their fighting skills, the ports had their own three law courts. The Court of Shepway was a court of justice dealing mainly with the Kent ports and was in place by the 12th century. The name 'Shepway', originally 'Shipway', is said to be derived from the Saxon word 'sceapwag', meaning 'path of sheep'. The name was also used for one of the medieval lathes (areas) of Kent and was revived in 1974 for the new

from duty], and lovecopefree [freedom to free trade]. And that they may have *Den* and *Strand* at Yarmouth according to the contents of our Ordinance thereof and for ever after to be observed.

The document was sealed with the corporate seal of the town, a Cinque Ports ship with a high stern and forecastle, with defensive bastions and one mast and yard with a large square sail. Inside the boat is a man blowing a horn and another is perhaps rowing.

The portsmen were renowned for their fighting skills and ruthlessness. In 1217 they prevented a French invasion by defeating the enemy fleet off Sandwich, and in 1242 were granted authority to harry and raid the French coast, which they carried out with

12.   The Corporate Seal of the town of Hythe, which features a Cinque Ports sailing vessel.

administrative district covering Folkestone, Hythe and Romney Marsh.

A Lord Warden of the Cinque Ports, who was also Constable of Dover Castle, was appointed by the king to preside over the Shepway Court, and this honorary office, which has been held by such notables as the Duke of Wellington, Winston Churchill and the late Queen Mother, remains in place today. The court dealt mainly with wrecks and piracy, and after originally meeting at Lympne (where the Shepway Cross now stands) usually met in later years at Dover.

The Court of Brodhull (later Brotherhood) was in existence by the 13th century to oversee the contentious privileges held by the ports at Yarmouth, which often led to open warfare with the east coast town. This court was held in the later Middle Ages at New Romney.

The third court was held at Guestling from the 14th century for the three Sussex ports of Hastings, Rye and Winchelsea. It was later combined with the Court of Brotherhood, and occasionally still meets. In addition to the general courts, each court had its own internal court of justice.

Hythe was always destined to be one of the smaller Cinque Ports. In 1229 the town was required to provide five ships, each with a master and a crew of 20 men and a boy, for up to 15 days of the year free of charge. This compared with Dover supplying 21 vessels, Winchelsea ten, Hastings six, Rye five, Sandwich five and Romney five. However, by this time the harbour was silting up due to the continuous eastward drift of shingle and Hythe was having difficulty in supplying its ship service. Following the Great Storm of 1287, the harbour became blocked by shingle and was only kept open with great difficulty. Furthermore, the French regularly attacked the town. In *c.*1295 a French prisoner named Sir Thomas de Tuberville was sent back to England to act as a spy and assist with a French landing on the coast at Hythe. He was to give a signal when it was time to land, but one of the five galleys landed its 240 men at the wrong time and they were all slaughtered. The other galleys, seeing what happened, fled.

Nevertheless, the tide had turned for Hythe as a Cinque Port and, as it retreated, times of trouble and strife lay ahead.

3
Times of Trouble and Strife

By 1335 Hythe could only supply three ships – *St Cross* (120 tons), *La Blythe* (100 tons) and *Waynepan* (80 tons) – and even these were of a smaller dimension than those supplied by the other ports. In 1341 the town could supply no ships at all and Edward III threatened to cancel the privileges of both Hythe and Romney if they failed to provide the required five ships. Four years later, however, in 1345 Hythe was able to supply six small vessels and 120 men for the Siege of Calais. Yet it was not just a case of Hythe suffering: the Cinque Ports as a whole were in serious decline during the 14th century and as early as 1306 the number of ships supplied to the Crown was reduced from 57 to 27 for a period of time. At the Battle of Sluys in 1340 the Crown had to pay for half the cost of the 21 ships provided by the ports. The French took advantage of their weaknesses and attacked all of the ports, with Rye and Winchelsea in particular suffering.

To compound its woes, Hythe suffered severely from the Black Death in 1348-9, and in 1400 was hit by a triple disaster when devastated by the plague, a serious fire that destroyed 200 homes, and the loss of most of its fleet and sailors when five ships and 100 men perished in a storm. The desperate townsfolk thought they were cursed and in 1412 it was recorded there were only 134 ratepayers left in Hythe.

Those who remained petitioned Henry IV for a new site for the town, but this was not granted. Ship Service was excused for five years and in 1414 Henry V released Hythe from its commitments as a Cinque Port. The town was rebuilt (a Wealden house at No. 67-9 High Street survives from this time), but an attempt to rebuild the harbour in 1412-13 with the aid of Dutch experts proved unsuccessful and it soon silted up again. When asked to supply a vessel in 1428, Hythe had to hire one from Smallhythe, near Tenterden.

A poignant reminder of the town's decline after the traumatic plague, fire and storms of 1400 may be seen in the nave of St Leonard's Church, where the later arches near the west tower were constructed on a smaller scale than their predecessors. The tower had been added in the 14th century along with a porch and pervaise to house the parish priest. Unfortunately it was weakened by an earthquake in 1580 and was brought down by another tremor on 24 April 1739. At the time of the collapse, ten people were waiting in the porch to climb the tower for a splendid view across Hythe, but to their good fortune they had been kept waiting while someone fetched the key!

The poor of Hythe were looked after at the St Bartholomew and St John Hospitals.

13.   An interior view of St Leonard's Church looking towards the altar, taken in May 1873.

14. St Bartholomew's Hospital, also known as Centuries, photographed in around 1880. This was later issued as a postcard in the Hythe Reporter series.

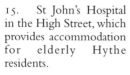

15.   St John's Hospital
in the High Street, which
provides accommodation
for   elderly   Hythe
residents.

St Bartholomew's was originally located at Saltwood, where it was named after St Andrew, before moving in 1107 to Centuries, Church Hill on the main road to Saltwood and Canterbury. Hamo of Hythe, who became Bishop of Rochester in 1319, is likely to have been born there in 1275 and on 11 May 1336 he was granted an almshouse charter for the building.

St Bartholomew's was endowed with an income of 20 marks per year, and each of the ten inmates received four pence per week. As a condition of residence they were required to attend mass and other services at the parish church, chant 300 Pater Nosters (Our Fathers) each day and pray for the founders of the hospital, and at other times 'should go about useful and honest occupations'. The hospital

was extended in 1811 but was closed in 1949 and converted into residences.

St John's Hospital, located in the High Street (then Kings Street), was originally an almshouse for lepers and from 1562 provided eight beds for the poor or those maimed in wars. In 1802 it was restored along with St Bartholomew's and it continues to provide accommodation for elderly Hythe residents, provided they can meet the criteria of being over 60 and a citizen of the town for at least ten years.

The later medieval years continued to see a decline in Hythe's status and, following the death of Richard III at Bosworth Field in 1485, the new Tudor age was to herald a great period in English history; but one which was largely to pass Hythe by.

4
Civic Pride and Prejudice

The Tudor age was to see the foundations laid for that great national institution, the Royal Navy, which, it could be argued, was the successor to the Cinque Ports fleet. Now that the harbours of the Ports were silting up and were all but useless (Hythe's consisting of only a narrow channel), the mighty warships of the new navy were to be constructed in specially commissioned Royal Dockyards such as Portsmouth, Chatham and Woolwich.

Hythe in contrast slumbered, but during the reign of Henry VIII (1509-47) the people of the town amused themselves by following the antics of Elizabeth Barton, the 'Holy Maid of Kent', at nearby Court-at-Street, Lympne, antics which scandalised the whole country. The Holy Maid was born at Aldington in 1506 and by the 1520s was employed in the service of farmer Thomas Cobb, who was bailiff to the Archbishop of Canterbury. At Easter 1525, aged 19, she became ill with a form of epilepsy that led to regular bouts of fits and trances. She remained in this state until the following November, when she predicted a child who was lying ill next to her would soon die, which he promptly did. During subsequent periods of delirium she spouted religious teachings and made further predictions, and declared that 'Our Blessed Lady directed her to go to the Chapel of Court-at-Street, between Aldington

and Lympne, and to make an offering of a taper there, and that she would be cured of her sickness.'

Elizabeth's prayers at the chapel led to an improvement in her health and people began to take notice of what she was saying. Richard Masters, the parish priest of Aldington, who had been responsible for obtaining Elizabeth's position with the Cobb family, heard her utterances and believed she was a saint. In collusion with a monk named Bocking, he reported his beliefs to the Archbishop of Canterbury, Warham, who appointed a commission to investigate the case. They were also impressed by Elizabeth's hallowed dictum and their favourable report led to her becoming a nun at the Convent of St Sepulchre's, Canterbury in 1526.

The 'Holy Maid of Kent', as she began to be known, continued with her divinations, encouraged by Masters and Bocking and recorded by the ecclesiastical historian John Strype (1643-1737):

> And to serve himself of this woman and her fits for his own benefit, he (Masters) with one Dr Bocking, a monk of Canterbury, directed her to say in one of her trances that she should never be well till she visited the image of Our Lady in a certain chapel in the said Masters' parish, called

16. The remains of Court-at-Street Chapel in 1829, drawn by George Shepherd and engraved by H. Smith. Very little of it remains today.

the chapel in Court-at-Street and that Our Lady had appeared to her and told her so, that if she came on a certain day hither, she should be restored to health by a miracle. This story, and the day of her resort unto the chapel, was studiously given out by the said parson and monk; so that at the appointed day there were 2000 persons to see this maid and the miracle to be wrought on her. Thither at the set time she came, and there before them all, disfigured herself, and pretended her ecstasies.

The Holy Maid even announced the impending death of Archbishop Warham, which quickly occurred in 1532 (yet as he was so old and worn out anyway it hardly came as a surprise). Elizabeth then turned her attention to Henry VIII's attempts to divorce Catherine of Aragon so that he could marry Anne Boleyn. Perhaps influenced by her spiritual advisers, the Holy Maid warned the King that 'many things that should follow to the world for punishment of the sins of the princes', and bluntly warned him that if he married Anne within seven months he would no longer be king. However, the marriage still took place in secret, at Greenwich on 25 January 1533, and then Henry went after those who had opposed the union. Cardinal Wolsey for one was indicted for treason (although he was to die on his way to trial), but this failed to halt the Holy Maid's criticism and she was arrested by Thomas Cromwell and forced to undergo public penance outside St Paul's Cathedral and confess her 'guilt'. She was tried for treason and sentenced to death, and was made to undergo further penance at Canterbury. On Monday 20 April 1534 Elizabeth was hanged at Tyburn along with five of her supporters (including Bocking, but not Masters who was pardoned) and when pronounced dead was drawn and quartered. Her fellow Kentish maid, Anne Boleyn, who had been vocal in calling for her death, did not survive for much longer, being beheaded on the orders of Henry on 19 May 1536.

Three years after the Holy Maid's death Archbishop Cranmer handed over Saltwood Castle to Henry VIII (who passed it on to Thomas Cromwell) and the Bailiwick of Hythe was leased to the town for 99 years. Following Cromwell's fall from grace, the Castle returned to the Crown for a short time before Henry's son, Edward VI, gave it to the Lord High Admiral, Lord Clinton and Saye. However, after suffering more earthquake damage in 1580, the Castle was left un-restored and was allowed gently to decay whilst in use as a farm.

During the reign of Henry's daughter, 'Bloody' Queen Mary I (1553-8), four Hythe protestants – Robert Streater, George Catmer, William Hay and Joan Catmer – were burnt at the stake in Canterbury. George Catmer had refused to accept the sacrament of the altar, claiming 'God is the worthy receiver spiritually, but the sacrament, as you use it, is an abominable idol.' He was burned chained to four other men, singing psalms until engulfed by the flames. His widow, far from being intimidated by her husband's violent death, took up the cause, but suffered the same fate the following year; those who witnessed it 'turned away their heads and wept'.

A survey of the Cinque Ports fleet in 1566 showed that Hythe possessed just a modest fleet of four 60-ton vessels, three of 30 tons and 25 fishing craft with 160 fishermen. The town was fighting a losing battle against the harbour silting up and in 1586 Camden in *Britannia* writes of Hythe, 'Its name signifies a port or station: though at present it can hardly maintain that name against heaps of sand which shut out the sea for a great way.'

However, for its last hurrah, the town did manage to supply the 50-ton *Grace of God* to combat the Spanish Armada in 1588 and gained a permanent reminder of that great victory in the shape of an old chest salvaged from a galleon. The chest was placed in St Leonard's Church and boasts a lock linked to a series of eleven bolts that is so heavy a lever is needed to turn the key.

During the 17th century final efforts were made to cut a new channel through the shingle into the old port but they were all doomed to failure. In 1615 a decree was announced and money collected for the 'cutting out of the haven', and in January 1619 the Corporation minutes record that the charges and labour of the work were to be borne by every 'particular ward within the libertie of this Town and Porte'. The harbour was reported to be just about usable in 1623, but in the following year another petition had to be raised. However, the work was stopped by 1627, when it was ordered that:

> all persons who had pay'd any money towards the effecting or obtaining of the haven here which are since that time dead or removed their dwelling out of this Town shall absolutely lose the said moneys in regard of the manifold great impositions and burdens lately imposed and put up on the inhabitants which reside among us.

Another scheme that failed was a sluice constructed in 1654 to release water from the high ground to scour away the silt, as did a final cutting in 1676. An earth bank constructed in 1682 to keep back the sea became known as Sir William's Wall and was later joined up with another bank called the Town Wall to form a fashionable promenade. The wall had largely disappeared by the 19th century, yet a few remains survived into the 20th century in the Recreation Ground.

By the end of the 17th century ships had no alternative but to unload at the Stade on the beach, now nearly a mile south of the High Street and old harbour. The marshy land of the dried out harbour that had accrued between the beach and the old town was reclaimed using earth bank walls strengthened with rods, and was leased out to private individuals who began to develop the area for residential and industrial purposes.

One Hythe guide romantically summed up the demise of the Cinque Ports, of which only Dover is a major port today:

For over four hundred years the Cinque Ports guarded the narrow seas, and fulfilled the whole duties of the Royal Navy. In the Ports was born and nurtured a race of seamen, bold, hardy and adventurous, disdainful of the odds against them, free and independent of spirit, but banded together by their communal life, and submitting to the discipline of their own selected commanders. They, first of Englishmen, adopted the true practice for defence of an island, namely, the engagement of the foe before he has a chance to land. It was of course inevitable that expansion would come, and owing to the growth of tonnage of the ships, and the silting up of their harbours, the Ports were unable to keep pace with the expansion. The spirit, however, remained

17.   An aerial view of Hythe from the 1930s. The location of St Leonard's Church in the distance gives a good idea of the amount of land that has been reclaimed since medieval times.

the same, and the incomparable seamen of the Elizabethan times carried on the tradition of the Ports. Even against the Armada in 1588 a squadron from the sadly shrunken Cinque Ports fleet fought under Lord Howard, and provided and manned the fireships, which did so much damage to the foe in the Calais Roads.

Yet, in replacement of its lost port, the town of Hythe had gained a new civic pride, fostered by the receipt of a Charter of Incorporation from Elizabeth I in 1575. The town was now able to elect its own mayor, along with 12 jurats and four common councillors, and hold a fair. In addition two town sergeants, two chamberlains, a town crier, gamekeeper, gaoler, pound keeper, billet master and hog driver could be appointed. St Leonard's Church has a brass plaque commemorating the charter above the grave of John Bredgeman, Hythe's last bailiff and first mayor, who was instrumental in securing the charter of 1575.

During the English Civil War (1642-51) Hythe was well away from the main scene of fighting and saw no significant action. The leaders of the town appeared to favour the Parliamentarian side, although William Brockman of nearby Beachborough led a rising for King Charles I in 1648 that was quickly put down.

In the year of the restoration of the monarchy in 1660 a Market Hall, later known as the Court Hall, was provided in the High Street, on the site utilised for the Town Hall in 1794. Five years later both the market and fair had to be cancelled because the Great Plague of 1665 afflicted the town. Ten years later the French still showed they were a threat when a man o'war fired 40 shots into Hythe on 26 May 1675 whilst in pursuit of a Dutch vessel.

Several buildings were damaged, including one of those belonging to brewer James Pashley.

In 1709 the Market Hall was the scene of the following complaint by the widow Mary Rand:

> On Saturday last she had stolen from her stall in the market place of this Towne, five pennyworth of Ginger Bread and that she hath in supposition, John, the son of John Partridge, who being brought before us and examined, confessed the said fact. Whereupon it is now ordered by the Mayor and Jurats here present that the said John Partridge be publickly whipped for the said offence.

As Hythe was a Cinque Port, two Members of Parliament had been returned annually to Westminster since at least 1322, with the voting strictly confined to those who held high office or considerable wealth. For example, in March 1689 Sir Philip Boteler and William Brockman were returned by just 16 voters, comprising the mayor, five jurats, six commoners and four freemen. Members and candidates were not afraid to use bribery in order to get elected or retain their seat. In 1710 the mayor Henry Deedes, was accused of assisting the election of Lord Shannon and John Fane by treating the whole of the Corporation to dinner at which he solicited votes. Leading the accusers was John Boteler, who had lost the election, yet he was not totally innocent himself: he promised one voter an interest-free loan of £20 or £30 over two to three years, while another was offered a bullock!

The Deedes family was one of the most influential in the town; for example, they were 22 times mayors of Hythe between 1640 and 1795. Julius Deedes was instrumental in rebuilding the tower of St Leonard's Church in 1750 and also reconstructed the south transept where he placed a private chapel. The family resided at the Manor House, erected in 1658 by John Deedes, who was three times mayor, an MP and Captain of the Trained Hythe Volunteers. The house, originally known as St Leonard's and facing the parish church a little way down the hill, was rebuilt in Georgian style in 1785.

Four years later, in 1789, William Deedes erected a new mansion at Sandling Park, on the site of an earlier house, designed by J. Bonomi. The house boasted 25 bedrooms, and fine gardens with an artificial lake. Jane Austen was once a visitor and was so impressed she used Bonomi's name in one of her novels. In 1942 the house was badly damaged by a bomb and was demolished save for the gateway and stone balustrade. Major Hardy erected a new red brick house in 1949-50.

The Tournay family were also firmly part of the fabric of Hythe. They were 19 times mayors of Hythe between 1712 and 1815 and Town Clerks for all but 12 years from 1705-1836. The family seat was Brockhill Park, Saltwood and Hasted's *History of Kent* relates: 'John Selling, of Brockhill, left an only daughter, Joanne, who carried Brockhill in marriage in 1498 to John Tournay, son of John Tourney, Merchant of the Staple at Calais, who was afterwards of Brockhill.' The son of John and Jane Tournay, who was also a John, married Bennett Honeywood. Their son, Thomas Tournay, donated the Hythe Moot Horn, bearing his name and the family crest, to the town in 1582. The horn was used to call the townspeople together for a 'moot' or meeting and is kept in the Town Hall.

The Moot Horn was also used in the ceremony to elect Hythe's mayor, being

18. The Old Manor House, erected in 1658 by John Deedes and rebuilt in Georgian style in 1785.

blown to summon the freemen, who elected the mayor and his deputy. The retiring mayor would then formally swear in his successor with the words:

> You shall be true and faithful to the King's Majesty and his Heirs and Successors and to the Commonality and Port of Hythe and the Franchises, Usages, Liberties and Privileges of the same. You shall rightfully maintain and keep to your Power, and the Common Profit thereof you shall have respect and regard unto; law and justice you shall indifferently minister as well to the Poor as Rich; and do all things uprightly so near as God shall give you Grace.

19. Sandling Park, depicted as Sandlands in this drawing by George Shepherd in the early 19th century.

20. The hunt gathers at Sandling Park on 8 January 1914.

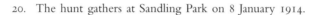

21.   Brockhill Park House, seat of the Tournay family, photographed by J. Weston of Folkestone *c.*1912. The building now houses a school.

Thomas Tournay's son, also a Thomas, was a Parliamentarian during the English Civil War and fell out of favour following the restoration of the monarchy in 1660. In 1903 the last Tournay owner of the estate, William Tournay, was buried with his favourite dog on the largest island in the lake. He had inherited the estate in 1883 but was a very private person, so it was no surprise to Saltwood villagers that after his death on 20 August 1903, aged 54, he was laid to rest on the island. Following the body's interment, all bridges to the island were destroyed, leaving Tournay and his dog to enjoy a very restful peace.

The Tournay family home is now part of Brockhill School, while the estate itself, including the island (which can still only be reached by boat), was opened by Kent County Council as Brockhill Country Park in 1986.

As well as representing Hythe in parliament, the members or 'barons' were expected to enhance the town in a practical way. Hercules Baker erected a new East Bridge in 1728 and 13 years later also provided new pipes to be laid from the town cistern. William Hales donated two maces for the town's sergeants in 1744; William Glanville built the church steps and provided a gallery in the nave in 1728. Under the Reform Act of 1832 Hythe's representation was reduced to one and the constituency was enlarged to include Folkestone, Cheriton, Saltwood, the remainder of West Hythe and a portion of Newington.

5
The Lure of the Sea

In spite of the decline of Hythe as a trading port once the harbour had been lost, fishing remained a principal occupation. By 1625 Hythe's fleet of ships consisted only of fishing boats, employing around 200 people. Salvage from wrecked vessels was an occasional profitable sideline for the fishermen, as in 1617 when two vessels *John* and *Ducalion* were stranded at Hythe.

The fish gathered by Hythe's comparatively small fleet was sold locally or sent to London. By the end of the 18th century fishing craft were flat-bottomed, so they could sit upright on the beach, and buff-bowed to stop them ploughing into the shingle as they were wound up onto the shore. They were either clinker-built, with the planks overlapped and clenched together with copper nails, or carvel-built, where the planks were laid flush and the seams were filled. The boats were open to the elements, powered by sails and had leeboards on each side that were lowered into the water to stop them being blown sideways. During the 18th century the lug rig (lugger) was developed; its simple standing lug sail needed just two ropes to work it, one to haul it up and the other to set the angle. More sophisticated variations such as the dipping (where the sail could be reset, allowing for more power) and gaff lug were developed, yet by the First World War many craft had been refined to become a two-masted rig. This had a large dipping lugsail with jib on the foremast and a standing lugsail with top sail on the mizzen mast. Usually there was also a staysail between the masts, and of course oars or sweeps, although by 1914 the boats had begun to be fitted with engines.

The two main kinds of fishing were drift netting for mackerel and herring, and trawling for flat fish such as turbot, plaice, brill, sole and dab. Mackerel drifting usually took place during the summer months and herring drifting in the winter, although those prepared to fish elsewhere could find them at other times of the year. For many years Hythe boats took part in the Yarmouth herring season, once the most important fishery on the British coast, while other craft fished for prized cod in the North Sea.

Another possible sideline open to the fishermen was smuggling. A rise in customs duties in the 1780s had made smuggling increasingly worthwhile, and during the Napoleonic Wars the duties were increased further, particularly on liquor and tobacco, to help finance the cost of the war. The picturesque Smugglers' Retreat in the High Street had a tower that was said to have housed a lantern to signal to smugglers at sea. The building fell into disrepair and was demolished in 1907-8.

22.   Shaking the mackerel from the nets on the Fishermen's Beach. A postcard issued by Parsons Library
*c.*1910.

23.   The High Street in around 1900, showing the old ivy-clad Smugglers' Retreat with its lantern tower for signalling
to the smugglers. The building was demolished in 1907-8. The Town Hall is visible in the background.

24. The *Duke's Head*, pictured in Edwardian times, with the landlord outside. Signs on the pub wall show that it offered a garage and good stabling and advertised Mackeson's Milk Stout.

25. An early 20th-century advertising postcard for the *Bell Inn*, stating that it was just five minutes from the sea, station and golf links. The proprietor, A.F. Ridley, also claims it was a noted port house.

The *Duke's Head*, dating from 1810 and once popular with farmers who frequented the market in Market Square (now Red Lion Square), is one of a number of Hythe pubs that have smuggling connections. Legend has it that a smuggler escaped the attention of the revenue men by hiding in a sewer beneath the inn. The *Bell* has an old smugglers' tunnel where casks of brandy and rum were floated through to the watermill behind. Contraband was also hidden on hooks in the attic and behind fireplaces, and the smugglers carved a foothold in the chimney stack so that they could climb up and use it as a lookout point. In 1963 two skeletons wearing boots, belts, hats and badges were found concealed behind a fireplace and are thought to be victims of some dastardly murder. Local rumour also has it that the weatherboarded timber of the house, said to be over 400 years old, was salvaged from wrecks in Dymchurch Bay in the days when the inn stood much closer to the shore.

In 1817 the Coast Blockade was formed to deal with the smugglers, yet it appears the practice became even more rife during the 1820s. A local customs officer asserted, 'As most of the inhabitants of Folkestone, Sandgate and Hythe are in the confidence of smugglers no information can be expected of them.' In August 1826 a patrol under Lieutenant Johnston came across a galley beached and being unloaded at Fort Moncrieff, and in the ensuing battle one man was wounded. Three years later one William Sampson was sentenced in Hythe to five years in the Royal Navy for smuggling 133 gallons of brandy and 34 gallons of gin.

The notorious Aldington Gang also worked this area of the coast during the 1820s. They were initially led by Cephus Quested, until he was hanged at Maidstone in 1821, and then by the farmer George Ransley, who also ran an unlicensed beerhouse called the *Bourne Tap*. Ransley organised his large gang in an efficient military manner to ensure that a cargo was unloaded with great speed while men with muskets kept watch. For example, at Sandgate in November 1820, 250 members of the gang unloaded a galley laden with spirits, tobacco and salt, and wounded three members of the Blockade force and captured another. The downfall of the gang occurred after they killed Quartermaster Richard Morgan at Dover on 30 July 1826. A large reward prompted informers to lead the Blockade men to Aldington and Ransley and some of his gang were arrested. Following their conviction, they were transported to Tasmania, and the end of the Aldington Gang marked the demise of large-scale smuggling in East Kent.

The formation of the Coastguard under the jurisdiction of the Royal Navy in 1831 led to the disbanding of the Coast Blockade. Reduced duties brought a decline in smuggling, yet it has never been entirely eliminated. These days, however, it is often people that are smuggled in. On one occasion during a winter in the 1970s three Pakistanis smuggled onto the Romney Marsh coast waited in vain at a RHDR station only to be told the next train was not due until April the following year!

Bouts of rough weather would find the helpless sail-driven ships left at the mercy of the sea. Some of the vessels wrecked off Hythe during this period include:

Nancy 14/1/1772 – Came ashore two miles westward of Hythe, although the cargo of rice and indigo was largely saved. The vessel had been sailing from South Carolina to London under the command of Captain Harford.

Diligent 12/11/1773 – Sailing from Marseille to Rouen under Captain Debau with a cargo of cotton when it came ashore near Hythe.

Vyhried/Vreede (formerly the *Melville Castle*) 23/11/1802 – Involved in the most tragic incident in the seas off Hythe, this was an old English East Indiaman of 1,200 tonnage with 32 cannon sold to the Dutch as a troop vessel. The ship had landed troops at Cape Town and took on military stores before proceeding to Batavia to collect goods. It sailed on 18 November 1802 and four days later the captain dropped anchor off the English coast in calm weather. An English pilot asked him if he would like to be piloted into port, but the captain refused. The wind began to increase in force throughout the day and that night a heavy storm caused the ship to drag its anchor until she became stuck on some wooden piling. Huge seas swamped the helpless vessel and the female passengers were put in shrouds for safety. However, thirty minutes later the *Vyhried* broke up, with the masts falling into the sea. Tragically, had the ship beached a further 200 yards east on an open stretch of coast many more lives would have been saved. As it was, 310 of the 318 passengers were lost (largely consisting of soldiers, their wives and children), as were 55 of the 65 crew.

Cleverly 17/1/1806 – Came ashore at Hythe while sailing from Ipswich to Bridport under Captain Hopley. The cargo was salvaged, although the vessel was lost.

Admetis 25/10/1808 – Driven ashore near Hythe and bilged with the loss of anchors and cables. Captain Craig had been sailing the ship with a cargo of coal from Sunderland to Exeter.

John and Margaret 23/6/1816 – A Sunderland vessel wrecked whilst unloading off Hythe.

Providence 1/10/1823 – Wrecked off Hythe.

The first Hythe RNLI lifeboat *Mayer de Rothschild* (in service 1876-84 with a record of five launches and no rescues) came into operation on 3 August 1876, having been donated by Miss Hannah Rothschild in memory of her father Baron Mayer Amschel de Rothschild, the town's MP between 1857-74. The boathouse at Seabrook, an ornate affair with turrets and gables, cost £550 and was immortalised as the 'Goose Cathedral' in Jocelyn Brooke's book of the same name.

In 1884 the generous Miss de Rothschild paid for a replacement boat, *Mayer de Rothschild (II)* (in service 1884-1910 with 20 launches, 27 rescued). The craft featured in probably the most famous of all local shipwrecks, that of the *Eider* and *Benvenue* on 11 November 1891, whose story has gone down in local legend. The small French schooner *Eider* had been sailing off the north-western coast of France with seven people aboard when it was caught in hurricane force winds and rendered unmanageable. The wind proceeded to drive the hapless schooner across the Channel until it was ultimately beached at Seabrook shortly after 7 a.m.

The captain and the crew initially decided to see out the storm by staying aboard their craft, but the continuing severity of the wind persuaded them to abandon this idea and they stripped off in preparation to swim the few yards ashore. As they stood on the deck in readiness, however, the schooner keeled over and threw them into the sea. The four crew members managed to scramble ashore, but sadly Captain Girode, his wife and nephew were drowned.

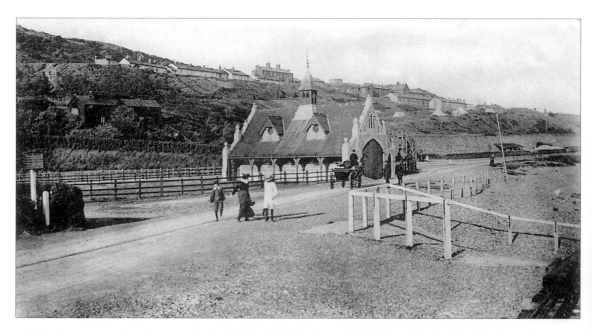

26. The ornate lifeboat house at Seabrook, dubbed the 'Goose Cathedral' by Jocelyn Brooke, pictured c.1901. The Hythe RNLI lifeboat was housed here from 1876-93 before it was transferred to Hythe. The building was demolished in 1956.

In the meantime, another vessel was in trouble in the same stretch of hostile water. The large three-masted full-rigged 2,033-ton vessel *Benvenue*, under tow on route from London to Sydney with a general cargo, had gone aground off Gloucester Place, Sandgate about 500 yards from the beach, causing her accompanying tug to cut the hawser. Her hull had disappeared beneath the waves and the crew were clinging on to the rigging for dear life.

Attempts to launch the *Mayer de Rothschild (II)* met with failure because the gales had washed away the slipway from the station at Seabrook. A decision was taken to launch elsewhere and, as fast as the horses could drag her, the boat was conveyed to Hythe. On arrival, hundreds of spectators lent many willing hands, which effected a successful launch of the craft containing coastguard Lawrence Hennessey as coxswain, 2nd Coxswain Albert Sadler, coastguard F. Fagg and Hythe fishermen Henry, William and Wright Griggs (brothers), J. Neal, T. Watson, E. East and E. Goodsell. They started off amidst loud cheers that soon turned to horror when the boat was almost immediately struck by a huge wave which overturned her. The crew were left floundering in the sea, yet almost all managed to scramble back into the boat, which had righted itself. The exception was Fagg who perished because he was a non-swimmer.

Frequent attempts were made to throw rocket apparatus to the *Benvenue* from the grounds of the Military Hospital, but each attempt ended in failure, as did attempts by No. 52 Battery Field Artillery, under Major O'Malley, to fire rockets from the seashore by a twelve-pounder breach gun. The lack of success was met with great frustration by the huge crowd, who were watching this heroic spectacle

27. The Hythe lifeboat *Mayer de Rothschild (II)* being pulled through the streets of the town in around 1910, perhaps on a fund-raising day.

with great excitement and some anxiety, in spite of being battered by gale force winds. To keep themselves warm, they lit great bonfires of broken wreckage along the beach. While all this was happening, the exhausted crew continued to hold grimly on to the masts, the only part of the *Benvenue* to remain above water.

As the wind finally began to abate around 5 p.m., the prominent Sandgateonians, the Rev. Russell Wakefield and Mr John James Jones, arranged with two Folkestone fishermen Bob Weatherhead and Dave Philpott to attempt another rescue. They managed to round up a further 14 men including Lawrence Hennessey and Albert Sadler (who were to assist Weatherhead and Philpott in conducting the operation) and Folkestone and Hythe fishermen Corrie, Freeman, Williams, Matthews, Mee, W. Griggs, Newman, Shelley, Fagg, T. Moore, A. Moore and Smith. At 9 p.m. the lifeboat was

finally launched and within 12 minutes had, amazingly, rescued all of the crew left aboard the stricken vessel to a crescendo of cheering from the relieved spectators on the beach. As a result of their valour, the local glory had been claimed, but only just, for the Dover lifeboat had arrived on the scene and almost wrested the laurels for itself. The Dover crew had been unable to launch when requested earlier in the day due to the bad weather, and, because of the exhaustion of the regular Hythe crew, the Folkestone fishermen were the only remaining option to carry out a rescue.

The rescued mariners were taken to Folkestone Harbour, where it was ascertained that 27 out of a crew of 32 had been saved. The five who had gone down with their ship included two teenage boys, washed off the deck, and the Captain, James Modrell, whose body was washed ashore some three months

28. The crew of the lifeboat *Mayer de Rothschild (II)*, comprising mainly Folkestone fishermen, who rescued 27 of the crew from the *Benvenue* on 11 November 1891. The photographer, Jacob of Sandgate, has captured them outside the Seabrook lifeboat house. *Back Row* (left to right): Corrie, Freeman, Williams, Weatherhead (2nd Cox), Matthews, Mee, W.Griggs, Newman. *Front Row*: Hennessey, Shelley, Fagg, T. Moore, Philpott (1st Cox), A. Moore, Smith, Sadler, Rogers (Signalman).

later. He was laid to rest in St Martin's Church, Cheriton. The inscription on his gravestone reads, 'Who lost his life while nobly doing his duty when in command of the ship Benvenue, wrecked off Sandgate.'

The surviving crew members, who had spent a total of 15 freezing hours clinging to the ship's rigging, received every attention during their stay at the *Queens Hotel* and Harbour Restaurant in Folkestone. Before embarking on the train to London they attended a special thanksgiving service at Folkestone parish church. The bravery of the lifeboat crew was rewarded by a £20 gift from Sir Edward Watkin, Borough MP and Chairman of the South Eastern Railway, and a commemorative medal approved by Queen Victoria. In addition Lawrence Hennessey was

awarded the Albert Medal Second Class and the RNLI Silver Medal. Albert Sadler gained the RNLI Silver Medal. The two men also received Lloyds Bronze Medals. Wright Griggs was similarly rewarded. In August 1892 Messrs Weatherhead, Philpott and other members of the rescue crew were awarded £195 for life salvage on the £14,400 of cargo recovered.

For a further ten months following the disaster, the ghostly spectre of the *Benvenue's* three masts continued to haunt the sea off Sandgate, until the vessel was blown up by a Whitstable salvage firm. Parts of the wreck, including a complete section, still survive to this day, along with some of its cargo of bedsteads, fireplaces, jars of herrings, jam and beers, wines and spirits. Just prior to its removal, boat trips

29.   A fine view of the western end of the High Street in 1872, little changed over 100 years later. The building on the left was where Francis Pettit-Smith, the inventor of the screw propeller, was born, and it was appropriately known as 'Propeller House'.

around the wreck were very popular and no doubt the passengers were enthralled with the graphic descriptions by the longshoremen of that dark November day.

On the recommendations of Lawrence Hennessey, the lifeboat station was transferred in 1893 to Hythe, where the boat could be launched more easily and the crew was closer to hand. A new lifeboat house was built on the Fishermen's Beach at a cost of £570 and the station at Seabrook was sold. It later served at various times as a bathing station for soldiers, a café and a private house before being demolished in 1956. In recognition of

the bravery of the Folkestone fishermen it was also decided Folkestone should acquire its own lifeboat station, which opened in 1893.

Hythe's association with the lifeboat also extends to a link with Lionel Lukin, who patented one of the first ever lifeboats in 1785. Born in Essex, Lukin spent the last ten years of his life in Hythe and following his death in 1834 was buried in the parish churchyard.

Another maritime progressive, Sir Francis Pettit-Smith, who is usually credited as the inventor of the screw propeller for steamships, was born at Hythe on 9 February 1808. He was the son of Charles Smith, for 40 years postmaster of the town. Following the successful introduction of the propeller to the SS *Archimedes* in October 1838, HMS *Rattler* became the first Royal Navy vessel to be fitted with one. Yet some dispute whether Smith was the inventor of the screw propeller, claiming a

Captain Du Vernet of the Royal Staff Corps had tested his version on the Royal Military Canal some fifteen years earlier. However Du Vernet died in Ceylon soon after the test and his achievement was forgotten when Pettit-Smith took up his ideas and advanced them.

6
Guardian of the Coast

❧❧

Following the French Revolution of 1789, the young Corsican officer Napoleon Bonaparte embarked on a series of wars against the European powers and in 1793 declared war on Britain. Peace temporarily returned after the Treaty of Amiens in March 1802 before war broke out again in May 1803 following a dispute over Mediterranean islands.

Napoleon declared, 'The Channel is but a ditch and anyone can cross it who has the courage. Let us be masters of the straits for six hours and we shall be masters of the world.' He assembled a large invasion fleet of 2,200 barges, fishing boats and other small craft, which were expected to transport 130,000 soldiers across the Channel once the British fleet had been lured out into the Atlantic.

To counter the invasion threat, it was decided to erect a line of defensive forts and towers on the vulnerable stretch of coast

30. The Royal Military Canal in the early 1890s, showing the third Ladies Walk Bridge to have been erected on the site. This bridge replaced the one washed away during the Great Flood of 1 January 1877, yet it was to perish itself in 1895 after collapsing at one end when crowded with people during the Venetian Fête.

between Folkestone and Seaford, along with a 28-mile canal from the eastern end of Hythe at Seabrook to Pett Level, near Hastings. On 30 October 1804 work began on what became known as the Royal Military Canal to the designs of consultant engineer John Rennie, but by May 1805 only six miles had been completed and the contractors were dismissed. The digging of the canal was then largely placed in the hands of Lieutenant Colonel John Brown of the Royal Staff Corps, who employed up to 1,500 men (both soldiers and civilians; the latter being paid 5s. 6d. per week).

The canal was dug to a depth of nine feet and was 62 feet wide at Hythe, although on the Romney Marsh it was only 30 feet wide in

places. Every 600 yards the canal was enfiladed to provide maximum firepower from batteries at each end, and was additionally protected by a 35-foot wide parapet with a banquette wall from which soldiers could fire at the enemy. The canal was also to be used to transport troops and supplies and had a road and towpath along its length.

The Duke of York opened the first section in August 1806, but the canal was not fully completed until 1809 at a cost of £234,310. Fortunately it was never put to the test against the French, who having crossed mighty rivers such as the Rhine would surely not have found 'Pitt's Folly' (as the canal was termed by its critics) too much of a problem. In 1810 it was opened for general navigation with a

31. Two of Hythe's surviving Martello Towers, Nos 14 & 15, that lie within the bounds of the Hythe Ranges.

regular barge service and a levy of tolls. The canal was stocked with perch and fishing, along with boating, became popular on the peaceful waterway. The War Office planted Huntingdon Elms along the canal bank in 1820 to provide the wood required for the old muzzleloader of the time. They were to be decimated by Dutch Elm disease in the 1970s. In 1877 the portion of the canal from Seabrook to West Hythe was leased for 999 years to Hythe Corporation. The remainder was leased to the Lords Bailiff and Jurats of Romney Marsh.

The defensive towers to be erected were the famous Martello Towers which are still a familiar feature of the coastline today. Their design was based on the French round tower at Cape Mortella, Corsica, which was attacked by the British fleet at the Battle of St Fiorenzo Bay in 1794. The tower proved to be a tough nut to crack and the garrison of 38 held out for two days as the cannonballs just bounced off the spherical walls. Lieutenant General Sir John Moore, who was attempting to land troops on the island, noted the effectiveness of the tower and later, in 1803, he took over responsibility for the English coastal defences between Deal and Dungeness. In conjunction with Captain W.H. Ford of the Royal Engineers (who had also fought at Cape Mortella) and Brigadier William Twiss, Commanding Engineer for the Southern District, Moore decided to erect towers of a similar design along the south coast.

Each Martello Tower was to be a circular elliptical structure 30-35 feet high with walls ranging in thickness from seven feet at the rear to 13 feet on the seaward side. They were armed with 24-pounder guns and could house one officer and 24 ranking men. Situated close to the shoreline, the towers were mostly spaced 600 yards apart so that the enemy would always be in range of cannon shot. The Prime Minister, William Pitt, approved the scheme in May 1804 and, it was said, personally selected the sites of the towers in Hythe.

Between 1805-10, 74 of the towers were erected between Folkestone and Seaford, 12 of them (Nos. 10-21) in Hythe. In addition, two redoubt forts were placed at Dymchurch and Eastbourne. Hythe also received three smaller forts – Twiss, Sutherland and Moncrieff – none of which have survived. Fort Twiss lay between towers 10 and 11 and boasted a battery of guns and accommodation for 100 men; Fort Sutherland was situated near Stade Street, and Fort Moncrieff was on the shore towards Dymchurch. In addition the Saltwood Battery was built in 1798 to defend the higher ground above the town. A further 29 Martello Towers were to be added on the Essex and Suffolk coasts between 1809-12.

However, like the Royal Military Canal, the towers never saw military action. After the ending of the war with Napoleon they were used as lookouts to combat smuggling, while others provided accommodation for the coastguards and their families. During another war scare with France in the 1850s some of the towers were temporarily re-armed, although a number were demolished early on or were taken by the sea. In 1940, when an invasion threat loomed large once again, the towers resumed a role as look-out posts and were armed with anti-aircraft guns and searchlights.

Out of the 74 south coast towers, 26 still survive, of which four (at Folkestone,

32. An unusual photograph of the seafront end of Stade Street in the 1870s showing Martello Tower No. 12 and adjoining properties that have long since disappeared.

33. A postcard view of West Parade in the 1930s, featuring Martello Tower No. 13 following its conversion into a house in 1928.

34. One of Hythe's broken Martello Towers, destroyed by the tremendous force of the sea. The sender of this postcard by W.S. Paine on 13 February 1905 states that the remains were blown up, although one piece was left standing.

35. A photograph of the Officers' Quarters at the School of Musketry, taken in the 1870s.

36. A group of musketeers poses for a photograph at the School of Musketry in June 1873.

37. The Hythe Ranges pictured in the 1870s, along with two of Hythe's Martello Towers. Note how bleak the area is, described at the time as comprising 'long deep shingle, tiring to walkers, and sadly windy'.

Dymchurch, Eastbourne and Seaford) are open to the public. The fate of Hythe's 12 towers was as follows:

No. 10 – situated by the *Hotel Imperial*, removed *c.*1877 for sea-front developments. The detonation of the tower broke many windows in the town

No. 11 – located off Marine Parade, close to present swimming pool, removed *c.*1878 for sea-front developments

No. 12 – junction of Marine Parade and Stade Street, removed *c.*1880 for sea-front developments

No. 13 – West Parade, converted into a house in 1928

No. 14 – survives on Hythe Ranges

No. 15 – survives on Hythe Ranges

No. 16 – lost, broken up by the sea by 1900 and blown up by the army *c.*1905

No. 17 – lost, split in two by a storm in 1913

No. 18 – lost, broken up by the sea by 1900 and the remains blown up

No. 19 – ruinous, fragments can still be seen

No. 20 – lost, ruinous by 1910

No. 21 – lost, ruinous by 1910.

The Napoleonic threat also led to the establishment of the Royal Staff Corps in the town, transferred from Chatham. They were housed in barracks erected in Military Road between 1805-10 until disbanded in 1838. In 1853 the barracks were occupied by the School of Musketry, specifically to train soldiers in the use of the new Enfield rifle, and firing ranges were laid out close to Hythe's western beach. The ranges were described in the *Illustrated London News* of 18 February 1860 as being:

long, deep shingle, fearfully trying to walkers who are not quite up to the mark, and about half a mile broad. It is sadly windy, and, as they are obliged to shoot towards the sea, there is no suitable background for the eye; but still, many first-class shoots are trained there. The eighteen foot target of General Hay, the Commandant, is a very prominent object, and on each side of it are ranged the targets for the men, with little cast iron huts, from which the effect of the shots is telegraphed by means of different flags, held in different positions.

The Wagon Train Barracks were also placed in Hythe during the Napoleonic scare, on a triangular piece of ground south of the canal between the *Duke's Head* and Scanlons Bridge. They were eventually demolished in 1839. During the Crimean War a Foreign Legion was accommodated in barracks on the slopes by Barrack Hill. Contemporary reports claim that their wives and children were housed in what were, basically, little more than mud huts.

7
Work and Worship

❧❧

One business that particularly benefited from the soldiers' arrival in Hythe was Mackeson's Brewery. Records of a brewery at Hythe date back to 1669 when James Pashley mortgaged his brewhouse for £50. From 1741 to 1802 it was held by the Friend family, maltsters from Ashford, who expanded trade by delivering their mild and small beer around East Kent. Upon the death of John Friend junior in 1802, his estate, including the Hythe brewery, was left to the three sons and daughter of Henry Mackeson of Deal. Henry and William Mackeson in particular became involved with the business and in their first year successfully bid for some land by the West Bridge in order to extend the brewery. Their enterprise soon paid off, largely thanks to the thirsty soldiers and labourers digging the Royal Military Canal. By 1820 Mackeson owned some 20 public houses in the area and continued to expand by acquiring local pubs and breweries, enabling a limited company to be formed in 1900. The world famous Mackeson's Milk Stout was first produced at the Hythe brewery in 1907.

The Mackesons acquired considerable status in Hythe and Henry Bean Mackeson was nine times mayor of the town between 1872-80.

38.   Mackeson's Brewery, home of the famous milk stout, as depicted in a Hythe guidebook. Dating back to at least 1669, the site ceased brewing in 1968 and the distribution centre was closed five years later, to be replaced by housing and a car park.

39.   A postcard issued by Mackeson's to advertise its most celebrated product, milk stout. The barrel has 'Hythe Brewery' marked on it and the milk churn boasts 'Each pint contains the energising carbo-hydrates of 10 ozs of pure dairy milk'.

In 1801 five public houses were listed in Hythe – the *Swan*, *White Hart*, *Red Lion*, *Kings Head* and *Duke's Head* – all later to become Mackeson houses (*The Bell* was at the time in the parish of Newington). By 1805 two others, the *Great Gun* and *Carpenters Arms*, had appeared. The two most distinguished pubs were the *Swan* and the *White Hart*, both situated in the High Street. The *Swan* was first mentioned in 1506 and was a popular coaching inn. A milestone set in the wall indicates that it was 12 miles from Ashford and 71 from London. This can still be seen, as can a Sun Insurance plate on the front of the building dating from the early days of the 19th century. At this time, to gain assistance in fighting a fire, your premises had to be insured with a registered company and display their badge. In 1807 the *Swan* started a packet-boat service to Appledore on the Royal Military Canal. The boat left once a day at 10.30 a.m., returning at 5 p.m., and ran until 1851 when the Ashford-Hastings railway line was opened. The pub's finest moment came in 1814 when Tsar Alexander and the Duchess of Oldenburg took tea there with the mayor, Richard Shipdem.

The *White Hart* dates from the 15th century, although the current exterior was added 200 years later. The pub contains a priest hole and once had robing rooms for the mayor with a connecting door to the adjoining Town Hall. The High Street is also home to the *Kings Head*, mentioned in 1583 as the *George* and later as the *Sun*, from which Sun Lane gets its name. Another Hythe pub that gave its name to a thoroughfare was the *Red Lion* in Red Lion Square (formerly Market Square). It was originally in 1670 known as the *Three Mariners* and later featured in Russell Thorndike's *Dr Syn* stories, but in 2000 the pub was controversially renamed the *Watersedge*.

Milling was another industry that became established in Hythe, largely carried out by the Horton family. Benjamin Horton (1775-1835) acquired Rockdene Mill through the will of his employer Stephen Brown, who had been killed by lightning at the mill in 1817. The mill, which stood in St Leonards Road and was of a white smock type, escaped damage by the lightning but was eventually demolished on

15 April 1835. However the iron wind shaft was still in place in 1944.

The Hortons also operated a post mill in St Leonards Road marked with the date 1617. The mill ceased operating in 1832 and was demolished in June of that year although without the permission of the Corporation who owned it. Benjamin's son (Benjamin) Joseph (1800-73), who carried out the deed, was required to erect cottages at 6-12 St Leonards Road in compensation.

As a replacement for the two lost mills, Joseph Horton erected Albion Mill in Windmill Street in 1835. From 1850 it was run using steam, but ceased operating in 1887 and was demolished in 1890. The mill cottages were still standing during the 1930s.

In addition, Hythe once had three other windmills. Stade Mill, Park Road was in

40.   The *Royal Oak* at Newingreen, a couple of miles outside Hythe on the main road to London, was a stop for the 'Rover' stagecoach that ran to Canterbury. This postcard shows the coach and inn in around 1905.

41.   The old Hythe Lower Mill, pictured in the 1890s after it was re-erected as Ashley Mill in Cheriton.

operation until 1902, and Cold Harbour smock mill, on the eastern side of Blackhouse Hill, was working before 1814 under the ownership of William Bassett. By 1821 it had been removed to Lympne, where it was burnt down in 1891. Lower Mill, a smock mill, was in the Cobden Road area by 1813, and in 1815 was acquired by the same Stephen Brown who was killed by lightning at Rockdene Mill two years later. The mill was up for sale in 1851 and ceased operating in 1858. In 1875 it was purchased for £150 by Mr Brissenden, a builder from Sandgate, who arranged for a Mr Spray of

42.   Seabrook House in around 1904 when the Horton family owned it. A housing estate now covers the site.

Folkestone to reinstall the mill at Tile Kiln Lane, Cheriton for £700. There it was run by Mr Gilpin between 1877-89 and then by W. Martin, who removed the sweeps in 1902 and installed a gas engine. The upper part of the mill was pulled down in 1919 and the remainder was bricked up. The old roundhouse of the mill back in Hythe was demolished in 1890 prior to the making up of Cobden Road, and the mill house followed suit in 1901.

Joseph Horton's son William Brown Horton (1839-1922) was involved in the acquisition of Horn Street watermill in 1874, and it remained in the family's hands until 1900 when acquired by George and Edward Swoffer. The mill was first mentioned in 1769 and in 1781 Austin Stace ran it as a corn and paper mill, using motive power supplied by either wind, or water from the Sea Brook diverted into a millpond. In 1822 the mill was being used for paper making

and by 1839 for seed crushing to produce oil. Power was produced by a large water wheel, 30 feet in diameter and the largest in Kent. Flour was subsequently produced until 1943 when the cogwheel attached to the water wheel broke and could not be replaced. The mill and its house were eventually acquired by Hawkinge builder R. Haggers for development and in August 1961 demolition was commenced by Dibble Bros. of Folkestone. However, while this was taking place, on 23 August a fire broke out in the mill and left it a charred ruin. The row of millers' cottages were not included in the sale and survive as private houses.

Hythe's earliest known watermill was Hevywater, or Evegate, Mill, situated at the bottom of Hythe Hill. In 1580 Martyn Allynson built a water mill in the vicinity of the present-day Rampart Road. The earliest known reference to Seabrook Mill was in 1512.

43. Horn Street Mill, which dated back to 1769, seen here when it was owned between 1900 and 1919 by George and Edward Swoffer.

By 1713 it was owned by the Honeywood (or Honywood) family, followed by William Wilkinson (1828) and George Paine (1837), who also owned nearby Horn Street Mill. The mill was in the hands of Mr Rubie when it was destroyed by fire during the early morning of 26 March 1859. The mill house still survives, but in spite of being a Grade II listed building it lies derelict.

The only surviving water mill in the town is Burch's Mill, Mill Lane, built in 1773 on the site of Damer's Mill and acquired in 1832 by George Burch, who ran a baker's shop and tea room in the High Street. The mill stands astride the Saltwood Brook, a 21½ foot-diameter mill driving four millstones. An auxiliary steam

engine was added in the mid-19th century after the millpond had begun to silt up. In 1932 the Burch family sold the mill, but the buyer Stuart Brown failed to keep it in order and, furthermore, it suffered bomb damage during the Second World War. Mr Brown died aged 100 in January 1982 and the mill was purchased by Tony and Anne Marston who undertook to restore it. From 1993 flour was milled there for visitors on open days.

The last member of the Horton family to be involved in the milling business was Frederick Bassett Horton (1874-1964). The family also ran a fleet of ships, including the *Crown*, *Vivid* and *Three Brothers*, involved in the coal and coastal freight trade. The Shipdems

44. A photograph of the Town Hall taken on a quiet morning in 1923.

were another Hythe family who operated colliers up to the north east.

The Tritton family was another group of local businessmen who were influential in the running of Hythe. Henry Tritton was nine times mayor between 1789 and 1813 and his son William held the office five times. Both had a hand in the building of the Town Hall in 1794, at a cost of £1,096, although William, a bricklayer and stonemason by trade, was largely responsible for the design.

The building was first proposed in 1791 and the finance raised with the assistance of Hythe's two Members of Parliament, William Evelyn and Sir Charles Farnaby Radcliffe, who both donated £100. Thomas Tournay, William Deedes, Richard Shipdem, Robert Finnis and Henry Tritton each gave £50. The hall was designed in a classical-style with Portland Stone Tuscan columns and an open space for a market. Originally a corn market, held on Thursdays, it was later discontinued in favour of a general market. In addition two large fairs were held every year: one, on 10 July, for cattle and another, on 1 December, for livestock and the exhibition of fat mutton.

The trading of people, it appears, was also conducted there. In 1805 the wife of one of the men employed in the digging of the Royal Military Canal was led by her husband to the market with a halter around her neck and tied to a post with a sign advertising that she was for sale. The woman was said to have been not more than twenty and a 'likely figure'. She was bought for sixpence by a mulatto, the big drummer of the 4th Foot Regiment, and led away.

An overhanging clock was added to the Town Hall in 1871 by Henry Scott, and further additions included a small holding gaol, replacing the one erected in Stade Street in 1801 (later Rock Cottage). In 1906 a dock and witness box were constructed in the council chamber so that it could be used as a police court, even though a purpose-built Sessions Hall had already been built in Bank Street in 1881 (later the Conservative Club, until destroyed by a bomb in 1942). A county court was held at the Town Hall until 1932, and Quarter and Petty Sessions until the 1950s.

In its early days the penalties handed out at the court were often severe. The town sergeant, John Mercer, was brought before the court for stealing and was thought to have been lucky to receive a branded hand rather than the sentence of death. Charles Igglesden, during one of his *Saunters Through Kent With Pen and Pencil*, records an account of a Hythe husband murder found among documents in an old oak chest in the Town Hall:

45. The Westfield building of the Elham Workhouse, erected in 1835. The date was commemorated in a stone tablet placed inside the building which could still be seen until its demolition in 1997 for new housing.

It appears that a Hythe butcher by the name of Lott fell in love with his maid servant. At that time, however, she was engaged to a man named Buss, who, however, being of a mercenary disposition, persuaded her to marry Lott upon the understanding that a will was made in her favour. The ceremony was gone through, but two days afterwards the trio went on horseback to Burmarsh and, after they had had a drink and rested at an inn, the bridegroom was taken ill. He died a few days afterwards and Mrs Lott, who had been arrested, confessed that while Buss had placed the poison in a mug she agreed to the crime. The two were found guilty, but sufficient time had not elapsed for a child to be born. The scene in court, when the young mother, holding her infant in her arms, was dragged from the dock at Maidstone, is described in the papers of the day in a most heartrending manner. Mrs Lott, who was quite young, and her accomplice were hanged on the same day and it is stated that a quarter-of-an-hour passed before she was dead. The fire was then lighted under her body and it was consumed to ashes.

At the other end of the scale from the wealthy Hortons and Trittons, the very destitute of Hythe were catered for at the Stade Street workhouse before (much to the relief of Hythe's snootier citizens) being transferred out of town to the Elham Union workhouse. On 16 May 1835 an order from the Poor Law Commissioners arrived at the Elham Union ordering the construction of a workhouse at Each End Hill, Lyminge, to cover an area of 43,676 acres and cater for 19 parishes (including Hythe and Folkestone). Edwin Chadwick, the first secretary of the Poor Law Commission, instructed that life in the workhouse was to be so dreary and unpleasant that it would be less 'eligible' or attractive than the lowest form of work, and men would therefore automatically be forced on to the labour market.

Work began on the construction of the workhouse in September 1835. The builder was Thomas Cozens of Canterbury, who had submitted a tender of £3,840. The workhouse was to include a chapel, separate male and female wards (for 400 inmates in total), a committee room, washroom and storeroom. Married couples were not permitted to live together or visit each other in their living quarters. The children stayed with their mothers or were sometimes placed together.

The causes of admission into the workhouse varied from childhood and old age to illness, desertion and unemployment. Vagrants, who usually wandered from parish to parish, were allowed to stay for three nights provided they carried out some work. Many of them would return to the workhouse again and again. The children were provided with schooling, which was amended in accordance with the various government acts that were passed in the latter half of the 19th century.

The first Governor and Matron, Mr and Mrs Nicholas Chubb, commenced their duties from 25 March 1836. The remainder of the staff consisted of a clerk (sometimes a local solicitor), a registrar, chaplain, schoolmistress, poor rate collector, relieving officer (who decided which paupers were entitled to the payment of relief) and ward orderlies. None of the posts was well paid and the turnover of staff was high. Later, as the workhouse grew, extra nursing staff, porters and a vaccination officer were employed.

A Board of Guardians was elected by the ratepayers of the parishes to superintend the work of the paid officials in the workhouse, and they were directly responsible to the Poor Law Commission. They met once a week to discuss all matters regarding the workhouse.

Each of the 19 parishes was initially charged for the expenses of its own inmates, plus a proportion of the central expenses accounted for by the guardians. Later, in 1866, all accounts were charged to the Elham Union, who divided the expenses among the parishes. Some of the more able-bodied inmates were entitled to 'outdoor relief' from their parishes, which on average was around £2 6s. per week for up to 14 weeks. This situation lasted until the passing of the Outdoor Relief Act in 1894, which authorised the guardians of St Mary's to grant weekly friendly society premiums to members of the Elham Union.

The uniform diet for the able-bodied inmates in 1835 was bread (6oz for men, 5½ for women) and cheese (1½oz) or butter (½oz) for breakfast and supper, and also for dinner (7oz bread, 1oz cheese) on the last four days of the week. On the first three days, suet and meat puddings (11oz men, 10oz women) and vegetables were served for dinner. The elderly in addition had 1oz of tea with milk for breakfast and supper, and the children bread and milk, with occasionally gruel. On Christmas Day, roast beef and plum pudding were served to the inmates, but this was abolished in 1850 owing to the expense. Later, bread and water were served for breakfast and bread and cheese with potatoes for dinner. A pint of porter accompanied the meal.

Most of the able-bodied men were put to work on the workhouse farm, while others broke up stones, ordered especially

46. Women inmates of the Elham Union Workhouse pose for a photograph in the early years of the 20th century. Note all the shawls, and the members of staff in the background.

47.   Seabrook Police Station and Courthouse, *c.*1905. Built in 1860, the buildings still survive in a somewhat dilapidated condition as a KCC landscape depot.

for the purpose. The women mended clothes and cleaned the buildings. All inmates were originally made to wear uniforms, although by 1850 they were allowed to wear their own clothes. They could be punished for any number of misdemeanours, ranging from uncleanliness, bad language and drunkenness to insulting a union officer. The punishment was usually a short spell of solitary confinement for the minor offences and an appearance before the Justice of the Peace for the more serious ones, which could lead to imprisonment. After 1900 the punishment for minor offences was downgraded to a withdrawal of tobacco and leave for a month.

The Elham Union continued to provide assistance to relatively large numbers of the poorer members of society. By 1914 public health in the workhouse had been greatly improved, and the regulations slackened, yet the food was still of a mixed quality.

The steady growth of Hythe during the Victorian era necessitated the provision and expansion of public services. Gas arrived in the town in 1844 when the Hythe & Sandgate Gas and Coke Company's gasworks were opened in Portland Road, later moving to Range Road. Electricity was provided from 11 November 1902 when, under the Hythe Light Order of 1900, an agreement for supply was reached with the Folkestone Electric Supply Company.

The Hythe Police consisted of just one constable when John Friend was appointed to the post in 1830. Four years later he was appointed Chief Constable at the rate of £5 per annum. This was increased to 12s. per week in 1844 when the position was made full-time. Yet the *Kentish Express*, for one, was very critical of the 'force', complaining in 1861, 'The Hythe force consists of only one constable paid 23 shillings and a penny per week, who "does as he pleases".' Friend was finally pensioned off in 1874 and by the following year Hythe Police consisted of a superintendent and up to six constables (three full-time) and, being independent of the county force, was under the jurisdiction of a Watch Committee. This was made up of the mayor and a committee of councillors, who had the power to appoint, dismiss or promote a police officer. The force continued to hold an unfortunate reputation during the 1870s, principally due to the fact its men were often found drunk on duty. One of the worst offenders was the superintendent, George Raymond, who used his position to obtain free beer from public houses in the town. In May 1875 the whole force was dismissed for insubordination and it appears

that between then and August 1875 Hythe was without a proper police force. Raymond was then reinstated, yet often remained in an intoxicated state, and was a bully to boot who had his colleagues dismissed on the same offence of drunkenness of which he was the worst offender. However, his luck ran out in 1878 when he was forced to resign by none other than Mr Mackeson, the Chairman of the Watch Committee, who owned the local brewery!

The Hythe Police were eventually incorporated into the county force in 1889, and in 1913 a new police station was opened at the junction of Sun Lane and Prospect Road. New cells replaced those at the Town Hall and were often used in preference to those at Seabrook Police Station because they were larger. The station was ultimately closed in 1996 and replaced by an office in the High

48. The Hythe Volunteer Fire Brigade was the first to be established in Kent, in 1802. This photograph shows them outside their station in Portland Road in around 1910.

Street. Hythe also once had its own ambulance station, situated in Bank Street.

Seabrook Police Station opened in 1860 and was enlarged with a magistrate's court on 20 February 1904. The building still survives in a somewhat dilapidated condition as a landscape depot for KCC.

The Hythe Volunteer Fire Brigade was the oldest in Kent, having been formed in 1802. By 1814 it had been renamed the Hythe Fire Engine Association, but in 1832 it split into two: the Corporation Fire Engine Brigade and the Scot and Lot Fire Engine Association, named after a form of municipal wealth tax. They were reunited in the 1860s and in 1866 became the

49. A Hythe Reporter postcard showing the burnt-out remains of the *Sportsman Inn*, High Street, destroyed by fire during the night of Sunday 2 June 1907. The Hythe Picture Palace was opened on the site in 1911.

Hythe Volunteer Fire Brigade again. At the time of the reunion Hythe was described as having a fire engine station with two engines for a population of 3,000. The writer goes on to say:

> The Association consists of 40 volunteer members, who give their time and subject themselves to fines for non-compliance to the rules, and honorary members, who pay a subscription of 4s. per year. The Kent office subscribes £5 per annum and the Norwich Union gives donations from time to time. The engines are two very old ones, for 20 men each, and are constantly requiring repairs to keep them in working order and there is 90 feet of leather hose for each engine. There is no fire escape in the town, but a long worn out ladder does duty as such. The supply of water in case of fire is derived partly from a canal running along the town, and from pumps, ditches and waterworks. The fires average about two a year.

A new engine was obtained at a cost of £173 3s. raised by public subscription. It could discharge 100 gallons per minute to a height of 120 feet. In 1885 the brigade was moved into a new engine house on the site of the old gasworks in Portland Road. The original building was reconstructed in 1925, but is now Hythe Garage, the fire station having moved to Wakefield Way. The old brigade was often hampered by a poor water supply and by 1900 the manual engine was out of date and inferior to Folkestone's steam engine. Hythe's own steam engine, *Speedwell*, was acquired in April 1905 at a cost of £260 with a capacity of 300 gallons per minute to a height of 150 feet. The firemen were summoned by the firing of a maroon rocket outside the station, and were horse-drawn until the First World War. In 1948 the station became part of Kent Fire Brigade.

The town's newspaper was the *Hythe Reporter*, first issued by Edward Palmer in 1890. Nicknamed the 'Ha'penny Rag', it ceased publication in 1949. The *Hythe Herald*, a sub-paper of the *Folkestone Herald*, and the *Kentish Express* now provide the local news for Hythe.

The local hospital for the area was the Royal Victoria, Folkestone, opened on 3 July 1890, which had a ward reserved for Hythe patients. 'Hospital Saturday' and 'Hospital Sunday' fêtes and parades assisted in generating funds for the hospital, which was maintained entirely by voluntary contributions until the formation of the National Health Service in 1948. A new general hospital for the south-east Kent area, the William Harvey, was opened at Ashford in 1979.

The Victorian penchant for church and worship led to the establishment of a number of churches and chapels in Hythe. The Ebenezer Chapel pre-dated the era, being opened by William Marsh in Chapel Street on 18 April 1814. However, it soon proved to be too small and was rebuilt to hold 300 people, the reopening taking place on 1 June 1817. In 1868 the congregation moved to the new Independent or Congregational Church erected in the High Street at a cost of £2,500. The old building was later used as a furniture store for the Hythe Volunteers' quarters, but was destroyed by a bomb on 10 May 1942. The Congregational Church itself also suffered bomb damage during the war and was eventually demolished in 1987, the congregation switching to the United Reform Church in Seabrook Road.

The Methodists erected a chapel in Rampart Road in 1845 for £60, which was replaced by a church in 1897. Smaller churches have included the Elim Pentecostal in Ormonde Road, St Michael's Mission Church (1893) in Stade Street, St Mary's Mission Room at West Hythe, the Victoria Hall in Victoria Road (now

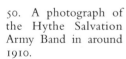

50. A photograph of the Hythe Salvation Army Band in around 1910.

51. A postcard showing the Catholic church as it appeared in 1912. The building had opened 18 years earlier on 6 August 1894.

housing) and the Salvation Army Hall (1903) in Portland Road. A branch of the Salvation Army in Hythe had been founded in 1895, largely at the instigation of fisherman Wright Griggs and his wife Elizabeth.

Father Chevalier opened the first Catholic Mass House in the town in 1854, yet between 1867-91 Hythe was without a priest and worshippers had to go to Folkestone. On 12 November 1891 Edward Selley established an Augustinian presence in Hythe and public mass was given in a lecture room in the School of Musketry and an old loft in Park Road. For the 'Feast of Our Lady of Good Counsel' on 26 April 1892 Father Selley leased the Temperance Hall, Park Road at a rent of £6 per annum. A site was acquired at Seabrook for a new church and a Mr Purdie of Harlesden

drew up plans, which included a school and priory. However, Father Selley resigned in September 1893 and the church was not built. His successor was Father Richard O'Gorman, who found a new site for a church and school at the junction of Lower Blackhouse Hill and Mill Lane. The church was opened on 6 August 1894, with the school following on 12 November 1894.

Father O'Gorman was also responsible for bringing the Ursuline Sisters to Hythe. They purchased a large house named *The Gables* in Seabrook Road and opened a fee-paying boarding and day school on 16 September 1895. As the number of pupils continued to rise, a bigger property was rented in Douglas Avenue, until the Northfields private school in Seabrook Road was acquired in 1901 to house

52. The Ursuline Convent was situated at Northfields, Seabrook Road from 1901-14, when the building was taken over by the Marist Sisters.

12 sisters and 40 boarders. On 8 September 1914 the Ursuline Sisters vacated the convent, which was taken over on the same day by the Marist Sisters, based in Fulham, London. Owing to the First World War, many of their early pupils were children of Belgian refugees. A new wing containing classrooms, concert hall and sleeping accommodation was added in 1930. Further expansion occurred in 1946, when the adjoining Villa Maria was acquired to lodge the junior school, and in 1950, when Cannongate House was purchased to provide residential accommodation for boarders to the senior school. However, Cannongate was sold in 1959 and the senior school closed in 1964. The junior school followed suit in July 1967, although the Catholic School of St Augustine's was transferred to the Marist

School on 12 January 1974. The Villa Maria and Fatima House were used as a children's residential home until 1982, but now house retired sisters of the order.

Restoration work to St Leonard's Church was carried out between 1875-87 by George Street and John Pearson at a cost of £10,000. The work included a new barrel-shaped roof in the nave (1875), a new pulpit (1875) and vaulting to the chancel and aisle roofs (1887). In the south aisle the poignant Hilyard Window commemorates 2nd Lieutenant Robert Hilyard, who was killed on the Somme. There is also a brass memorial to Edward Colley, who died aged 37 on the *Titanic* in 1912. Newer additions include an East Window (1951), depicting Hythe's role in the defence of England, and a choir vestry on the north side (1959). Both

Saltwood and Lympne churches also received some form of Victorian restoration.

St Leonard's Church of England School dates back to July 1814 when it was known as the Hythe National School and was located in the High Street at Captain Robinson Beane's house. Captain Beane was ten times mayor of Hythe between 1671-96. The building was leased from General Kenneth MacKenzie at a rent of £13 per year and 82 boys were admitted after their parents had paid 1d. for a week's schooling. Girls were allowed to attend from 1817, and by 1843 there were 140 boys and 82 girls on the register. In the following year the school was forced to move after refusing to pay for repairs to the building. They were re-housed in the disused workhouse in Stade Street (leased at an annual rent of £15), before a new school was built on the old Ordnance Yard, St Leonard's Road. The Archbishop of Canterbury officially opened this

on 2 December 1851. In 1909 a further building was added which is now used exclusively by the juniors, a new infants school (the Hythe Community School) being built in the 1950s at Cinque Ports Avenue. In 1954 senior school education in Hythe was reorganised with the opening of St Leonard's County Secondary School for Girls at St John's Road, Saltwood and Brockhill Secondary School for Boys. Eventually, in 1978, the two schools were amalgamated. In the western part of the town Palmarsh gained its own infant and junior school.

A number of schools have also stood on Seabrook Road. There was the imposing white façade of the Seabrook Lodge Special Residential School for Boys, the Seabrook Hall School for Girls, the Pinehill Pre-Preparatory School, as well as that at the Ursuline/Marist convent. Currently there is Foxwood, a special school for children. At 4 Douglas Avenue was

53. Polden & Hogben of Folkestone captured this interior view of St Peter & St Paul's Church, Saltwood in around 1910.

the establishment of Misses Rigden, for 'daughters of gentlemen' (also at Fairview, Tanners Hill), and Mr Bertram Winnifrith had a long established school at Prospect House and then Beaconsfield House, Marine Parade.

In 1886 the prosperous Mayor of Hythe, Thomas Judge, presented an ornate drinking fountain to the town, which was placed in the wall of Dr Fagge's premises adjoining the Town Hall. Sculptured by Wills Bros using iron from the famous Coalbrookdale Ironworks, the fountain commemorated the biblical story of Moses striking a rock to bring forth water as the Israelites made their way from Egypt to the Promised Land. Psalm 41 is quoted on the fountain, 'He opened the rock and the waters gushed out. They ran in dry places like a river,' and figures of Moses and baby Moses with

54. Hythe National Schools, St Leonard's Road, pictured on a Hythe Reporter postcard c.1903.

his mother Miriam amongst the bulrushes are depicted. Dr Fagge's house became a bank in 1889 and when that was enlarged in 1911 the fountain was removed to Red Lion Square, where it still stands.

The High Street has always been the principal shopping area in Hythe and was home to a number of long-established businesses.

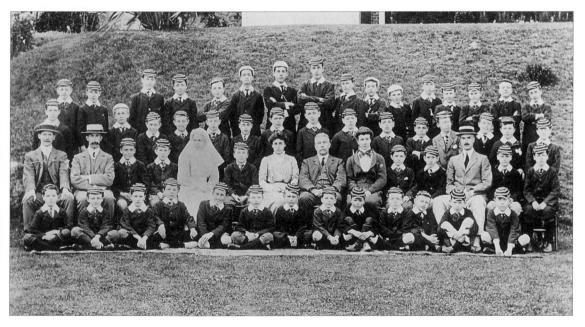

55. The pupils and staff of Seabrook Lodge School for Boys posing for a photograph in 1909 when H. Strahan was headmaster. This was a private boys' school for the education of 'gentlemen's sons'.

56. The staff and pupils of Stone House Girls School, Saltwood in 1914.

57. The 1st Hythe Scout Troop photographed in around 1911. The scouts had been established in Hythe three
years earlier.

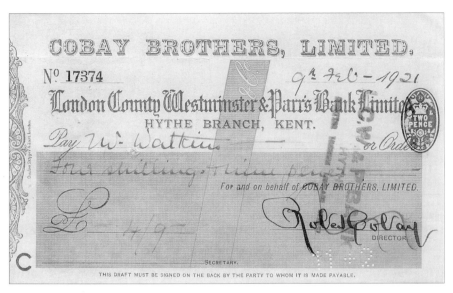

58. A cheque written out for 4s. 9d. by the long established Hythe firm of Cobay Brothers in 1921.

59. The staff of the International Stores outside the shop at 157 High Street (now 43 & 45) in 1908. The Hythe branch opened in 1898 and remained on this site until 1973.

60. The General Stores at No. 1 Devonshire Place, Horn Street was opened in 1912 by Joseph Wellings, but by 1915 it had become a private house.

For over one hundred years from the 1820s to the 1930s the Cobay Brothers traded as auctioneers, estate agents, house furnishers and undertakers. The brothers also had a big hand in the affairs of Hythe. George was mayor in 1881-2, as was Henry in 1887, 1896 and 1897, Robert in 1911 and William throughout the First World War.

Prior to the arrival of the supermarket (the first, Fine Fare, was opened in 1966), general stores flourished in the High Street. They included the Home & Colonial Stores (1910-62), Richard Price/World's Stores (1888-1968), International Stores (1898-1986), the Co-op (1907-84) and Vye & Son/Lipton's (1936-86). Other long-running concerns included Lovicks the stationers and Blundens bootmakers. Two firms still trading in the High Street after many years are Eldridges (said to date back to the 18th century) and Walter & Son shoe shop, founded in 1849.

In addition to the *Swan*, *White Hart* and *King's Head* already mentioned, the High Street also boasted a number of other public houses. The *Globe* remains open, but long gone are the *Sportsman* (burnt down 1907), *Providence* (closed 1911), *Cinque Ports Arms* (1962), *Rose & Crown* (1971) and *Oak Inn* (1980).

8
A Genteel Watering Place

Hythe was recommended as a good bathing place as early as 1782 when Seymour commented, 'The shelter afforded by the hills from the north and east winds and the mildness of the sea breezes on the shore invite a very early attendance of bathers in the spring and encourage them to protract their stay further into the autumnal season than is usual elsewhere'. In addition, he recalled:

Hythe consists chiefly of a long street, wide, and adorned with some good buildings. Travellers meet with good accommodations and convenient vehicles at the *White Hart* and *Swan Inn*. A hoy goes to and from London every month with goods and passengers, and boats are employed whenever the weather permits to catch fish. The town is too great a distance from the sea for great foreign trade. The mail arrives by way of Dover at half past nine and proceeds to Romney, returning at half past three.

In 1760 the Hythe-New Romney road was turnpiked, the tollgates standing where the present *Gate Inn* now stands. A rhyme on the inn sign exhorted, 'This gate hangs high and hinders none, refresh and pay, and travel on.' Where the New Romney and Ashford roads diverged was known as Gallows Corner

because Hythe's gibbet was situated there. The improved access to the town encouraged more visitors, including the Hon. John Byng on his great tours of England between 1780-90. He came to Hythe via Westenhanger and commented:

This is a good station for sea bathing and retirement, for rides up the country are shady and pleasant. We now walked together to the Battery on the beach, which might prevent the approach of a Privateer. Our dinner consisted of herrings split – and the roes lost – odd cookery this, with beef steaks, which is always a tough business. Port wine not drinkable. One starves in a tour, but in this, with the air and the exercise, consists of salubrity. After dinner, quitting Hythe, we rode up a lane of one mile to Saltwood Castle. The prospect from it is very beautiful. This noble ruin, the best I ever saw, is but little noticed or visited.

The prominent mention of food by Byng is hardly surprising for the people of the time had huge appetites. More people died of overeating than starvation and they continually partook of rhubarb and 'vomits' to make room for more. A typical fare for a club meeting in the 18th century would be a couple of rabbits smothered in onions, a neck of mutton boiled, a goose roasted with currant pudding and a plain one. In the afternoon everyone drank tea and then played pool or quadrille; a glass or two of punch was also partaken before everyone went home. The tea was usually obtained from smugglers, as were the spirits. A tub of gin, containing 19 bottles, cost £1 6s. and half an anker of rum was £1 15s.

Byng's mention of sea bathing was no surprise for by this time it was becoming increasingly popular, notwithstanding the fact that before 1750 most British people had regarded the sea with some hostility. Agreed, it acted as a defensive barrier for the island and provided food, yet it was also dangerous, unpredictable, and a graveyard for the nation's seamen and fishermen. Coastal villages and towns tended to turn their backs on the sea and the beach was no more than a gathering place for food and the means of getting into a boat. During the 17th century, however, there had been a re-emergence of the Roman practice of bathing in and drinking of the mineral rich waters at spas. One of the most popular of the spas, Scarborough, was on the coast and in 1667 the town's Dr Robert Wittie of Scarborough Spa also recommended the bathing in and drinking of seawater (or 'Neptune's Ale' as it was termed) to cure gout and kill all worms. The breathing in of ozone in the sea air was also good for health.

The subject of bathing was first written about in English by Dr William Turner in 1562 in *A Booke of the Nature and Properties of the Bathes in England, Germany and Italy*. Further thoughts on the subject were published by Sir John Floyer in his *An Enquiry into the Right use and Abuses of the Hot, Cold and Temperate Baths in England* (1697) and *A History of Cold Bathing*

(1702). Sea bathing really took off, however, with the publication in 1752 of Lewes doctor Richard Russell's *Dissertation on use of Seawater*. One of his cures rather unappetisingly consisted of 'a pill compound of some or all of crab's eyes, burnt sponge, vipers flesh, cuttlefish bones, tar and tincture of wood lice taken at night, with a pint of seawater in the morning'. Slightly less unappetising was the Rev. John Wesley's recommendation in his *Primitive Physic* (1776) that you drank seawater every morning for a week and bathed daily in the nude during the early morning when the sea was colder.

Russell's treatise led to Brighton becoming a fashionable resort, whose status was further enhanced when the town was frequented by the Prince Regent from 1783. Scarborough, Weymouth and Margate were other early resorts, and they imitated the spas by offering the same pleasures – baths, assembly rooms, ballrooms, theatres, circulating libraries – but with the added benefit of sea water and ozone.

W.H. Ireland was an early 19th-century visitor to Hythe and recorded:

The High Street is capacious, perfectly level, handsomely built and conveniently paved. Near the centre on the northern side stands the Guildhall and market place, a commodious structure rebuilt at the expense of the Corporation in 1794.

Hythe contains some good and spacious inns, a subscription reading room and excellent public library. The shops, as well as the dwellings, belonging to the superior classes of the inhabitants, bespeak the opulence, respectability and commercial importance of this place.

There are many pleasant houses upon ledges of the cliff above the town, commanding delightful and extensive views both of the sea and the neighbouring country, as well as numerous convenient habitations appropriated for the use of strangers during the bathing season.

Others are occupied by the families of officers of rank in the army stationed at this place, who greatly contribute to enliven and improve the society constantly frequenting the town.

However, the caustic radical MP William Cobbett was not so enamoured of Hythe when he visited the town during one of his famous rural rides in 1823. He declared:

Hythe is half barracks; and barracks most expensive, most squandering, filling up the side of the hill. All along the coast are some works of some sort or another; incessant sinks of money; walls of immense dimensions; masses of stone brought and put into piles. Then you see some of the walls and buildings falling down; some that have never been finished.

The Royal Military Canal was dismissed by Cobbett as being 'made for the length of thirty miles to keep out the French; those armies who had often crossed the Rhine and Danube, were to be kept back by a canal, made by Pitt, thirty feet wide at the most!' On the subject of the Martello Towers Cobbett was particularly scathing:

I think I have counted along here upwards of thirty of these ridiculous things, which, I dare say, cost five, perhaps ten thousand pounds each. These towers are now used to lodge men, whose business it is to sally forth not upon Jacobins, but upon smugglers. Thus after having sucked up millions of the nation's money, these loyal Cinque Ports are squeezed again, kept in order, kept down by the very towers,

which they rejoiced to see keep down the Jacobins!

One of the earliest venues for entertainments in Hythe was the Town Hall, yet the town also boasted its own theatre for a time, built at a cost of £400 and completed by 1804. The theatre was situated in Back Lane, a small thoroughfare off the High Street that was later renamed Theatre Street. The owner was Thomas Trotter, who held others at Worthing, Southend and Gravesend. Trotter divided his time between his various theatres and during his absence touring companies were invited to keep them open and raise revenue. On 13 March 1809

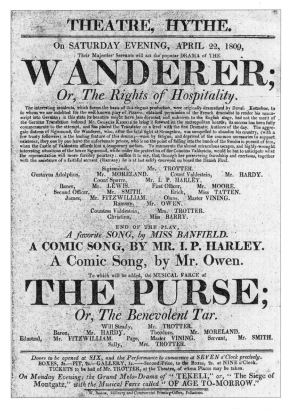

61. A poster advertises the Hythe Theatre's production of *The Wanderer* on Saturday 22 April 1809. The owner of the theatre, Thomas Trotter, is playing the lead role of Sigismond.

62.   The macabre collection of skulls and bones, probably of Black Death victims, displayed in the crypt of St Leonard's Church. The photographed scene was around 1900, but remains little changed today.

Trotter was at Hythe performing Sheridan's *The Rivals*, along with a Miss Banfield who sang for the audience after the play. He was still at Hythe the following month as a poster survives for a performance of the comedy *The Soldier's Daughter* on 19 April 1809, with Trotter playing the part of Frank Heartall. The evening's entertainment, which commenced at 7 p.m., also involved a comic song by Mr I.P. Harley, the ballet dance *Apple Stealers* and the musical farce *Lock and Key*. Prices ranged from 3s. (boxes), 2s. (pit) and 1s. (gallery) with boxes available at 2s. from 9 p.m.

However, thanks to the success of his Worthing Theatre, Trotter decided to concentrate his efforts on Sussex (he also leased Brighton's

Theatre Royal from 1814-19) and his theatres at Southend and Hythe were closed in 1812 and 1813 respectively. For the next 13 years the Hythe Theatre appears to have remained largely closed. On 1 May 1826 it was sold at auction at Covent Garden for £480, the purchaser Henry Roxby Beverley paying half in cash and the remainder by mortgage. A surviving playbill shows that Beverley gave a performance of *Saltwood Castle 1649* at the theatre in October 1827, but in 1831 the mayor's bailiff closed it

63.   Ladies Walk in the 1870s, a delightful tree-lined promenade extending from the town to the sea. The photograph was captioned 'Lovers Walk' although the walk was also known as Marine Walk or Victoria Walk.

down. Beverley never completed payment on the property as it was still in the hands of Trotter's trustees upon the latter's death in 1851.

In 1847 Bagshaw's *Kent* directory reported that the theatre had not been used since 1837 and was in such a state 'the roof had fallen in from decay and neglect – the interior is one mass of ruin and dilapidation'. The building spent some time as a furniture store, but by 1857, when Henry Dray acquired the site, it had been cleared away.

Among early attractions for visitors were circulating libraries, which, aside from being reading rooms, were places to meet and socialise. Roden's Circulating Library was in business at Folkestone from 1806-11, before moving to

Hythe in August 1811. However, Roden was declared bankrupt in late 1814 and his stock was sold by auction in January 1815. William Tiffen took over Roden's business in Folkestone and also had a branch in Hythe; he was among the first to publish seaside guides for the district.

A poster also exists for two days' horse racing held at Hythe on 1-2 June 1813. A most fashionable attraction of the time, and still a notable curiosity, was the macabre collection of 2,000 skulls and 8,000 thighbones housed in the ambulatory (or crypt) of St Leonard's Church. They are thought to be medieval in origin and may include victims of the Black Death disinterred to make way for new graves as the churchyard filled up. Others have claimed

64.   One of the earliest photographs of Hythe, taken in the 1850s. Where the man is standing by the old Town Bridge is now busy Stade Street.

65.   Hythe's tentative bid to become a seaside resort was boosted with the opening of this fine indoor bathing establishment in 1854. By the time of this 1920s postcard, the building was known as the Pavilion and was in use as a tea room.

the remains are those of Saxons, either killed in a great battle in 456 or against the Danes in 843.

During the Georgian period Hythe slowly gained a hold as an embryonic seaside resort, the population rising from 1,240 in 1801 to 1,987 in 1811. In the *Hythe, Sandgate and Folkestone Guide* (1816) it was stated:

> In the immediate neighbourhood of Hythe there is a pleasant walk called the Marine Grove, leading to the sea-side, and another denominated Sir William's Wall, where both visitors and the inhabitants frequently form agreeable promenades (especially in the summer evenings), and to which the refreshing coolness of the sea-breezes are extremely inviting.

Marine Walk was more popularly termed Ladies Walk, and was a fashionable tree-lined promenade that led from the Royal Military Canal to the seafront. The walk was first laid out in 1810 to commemorate the Golden Jubilee of George III and was particularly favoured for Church Parade, where the wealthy strolled along the walk after Sunday service showing off all their finery.

However, the arrival of Hythe as a respectable watering place really began in 1854, when the Corporation opened the Bathing Establishment behind the sea front in South Road at a cost of £2,000. The baths, a remarkable classically influenced building, boasted a distinctive dome that was based on the grand spa buildings at Bath and Cheltenham. They catered for the craze amongst the wealthy that the bathing in, and drinking of, seawater could cure all their ills. Indoor baths had grown in popularity as a more comfortable alternative to sea bathing whilst, unsurprisingly, the drinking of seawater was in decline by 1860. However,

66.   A general view of Hythe Esplanade taken from West Parade by Valentines, *c.*1900. Features of interest include the Bathing Establishment, donkeys, bathing machines, boats for hire and the boy with the yacht.

67.   Children paddling in the sea off Marine Parade are delightfully captured around the time of the First World War by Folkestone photographer Hawksworth Wheeler. Notice how nearly everyone is wearing hats!

the recommended daily dose for any partakers was ½ pint of seawater mixed with milk, beef tea or port wine. The said benefits were an easing of acute and chronic rheumatism, gout, consumption, asthma, indigestion, diseases of the liver, scrofula, rickets, measles and whooping cough.

Hot and cold baths could be had at the Hythe establishment for 6d. and also available was traditional bathing from bathing machines. The bathing machine, one of the few distinctive features of the Victorian seaside to have disappeared completely, first saw the light of day at Scarborough in 1736. These elegant, if rather clumsy, machines were basically a changing room on wheels, with a door to go into from the beach and another at the front to enter the sea. A modesty hood, invented by the Margate Quaker Benjamin Beale in 1753, was sometimes added at the front to protect bathers from prying eyes as they entered the water. The machines were hauled to and from the sea over Hythe's steeply shelving shingle beach either by horses or by using a winch.

Patrons to the baths could also partake of a refreshment room, reading room and boat trips around the bay. In 1892 James Cumming, 22 years an attendant at the baths, erected bathing tents in the vicinity of the *Seabrook Hotel*. The tents were by now succeeding the cumbersome bathing machines; they in turn were replaced by bathing huts from the 1920s. The price for tent, bathing costume and towels was 3d., for bathing from a boat 6d. and for boats (per hour) 1s. Visitors' own tents were erected, and swimming was taught before eight o'clock. Pure seawater was delivered to any home in Hythe at 1d. per can.

However, as was the case with many nascent watering places, it was the arrival of the railway that was to kick-start Hythe's development as a seaside resort, enabling the town's population to grow from 2,675 in 1851 to 6,387 by 1911. The railway was promoted by the South Eastern Railway (SER) and the first sod was cut by Prince Arthur of Connaught, grandson of Queen Victoria, on 11 April 1872. The line was opened by

68. A view of Sandgate Station in 1891, which straddled the Sandgate-Hythe boundary and was nearer to Seabrook than Sandgate. The station building is a typical South Eastern Railway clapboard structure that was demolished following the station's closure in 1931.

HRH The Duke of Teck on 9 October 1874 and trains ran from Westenhanger on the main London-Folkestone line through Hythe to a station named Sandgate, although it was actually nearer to Seabrook. On New Year's Day 1888 a new station was opened where the branch deviated from the main line at Sandling Junction. The branch was envisaged as a new through-route to Folkestone Harbour, but local opposition ensured this never happened and it became a quiet backwater.

In the year the railway opened, 1874, its chief promoter, SER Chairman Sir Edward Watkin, was elected the Member of Parliament for Hythe. He was to hold the seat until 1895 and died six years later at the age of 82. Sir Edward, who was also a director of the Metropolitan and Great Eastern railways as well as several other concerns, was a man of great dreams and schemes, many of which unfortunately never came to fruition. Aside from the through-route to Folkestone via the Hythe branch, they included a Channel Tunnel (quickly abandoned), a Grand Canal for Ireland (never started) and an Eiffel Tower for London. The first stage of the tower was built and opened to the public, but the rest of it failed to materialise and 'Watkin's Folly', as it was derided, was eventually dismembered between 1902-7.

The year 1874 also saw the Borough of Hythe extended to take in parts of the parishes of Newington (which extended down through Burch's Mill to the shore by the *Seabrook Hotel*) and portions of Saltwood and West Hythe. On 25 March 1886 the eastern part of Seabrook,

69. Sandling Junction Station in around 1900 with an Ashford-bound local service on the main line and a train in the Hythe branch platform.

formerly in the parishes of Cheriton and Sandgate, was annexed to Hythe.

Following the opening of the railway and the prospect of an increase in visitor numbers, Hythe Corporation turned their attention to the development of the sea front. Between 1875-7, in partnership with the Hythe Land & Building Investment Company, they laid out a promenade and sea wall. Safe and clean bathing was ensured with the laying of a 1½-mile waste water outfall pipe in 1876 by Mr Brady, Engineer for the SER. Select residences were erected beside the promenade, some of them as boarding houses for visitors. Saltwood Gardens and Beaconsfield Terrace were further additions in the 1880s, and between 1889-90 West Parade was laid out and furnished, with Rostrevor Terrace and Ormonde Terrace. In June 1896 two most attractive oriental-styled shelters were erected between Saltwood Gardens and Beaconsfield Terrace.

The South Eastern Railway were also prepared to take a hand in the development of the resort and on 21 July 1880 opened the *Seabrook Hotel* on Princes Parade at a cost of £30,000. The hotel was developed as part of the Seabrook Estate that was to include high-class villas and terraces and a pleasure pier, all of which failed to materialise. Princes Parade, however, was developed for a length of 6,000 feet to the Sandgate boundary, and was officially opened on 15 October 1881 by their Royal Highnesses The Prince of Wales and The Duke of Edinburgh. A new wing was added to the hotel on 25 April 1896, but the SER struggled to make it pay and the building was acquired in 1901 by the Hythe Imperial Hotel Company, led by William Cobay, who duly renamed it the *Hotel Imperial*. The company carried out extensive refurbishments and upgraded the hotel to offer 120 bedrooms, a large dining room, a lounge, smoking, reading and billiard rooms and a ten-course 'Imperial Table d'Hote' dinner. The extensive grounds featured Grand Fancy Fairs and Military Fêtes, bicycle gymkhanas, donkey derbies and rifle shooting. The hotel liked to claim that Hythe had the lowest death rate in England (a very persuasive selling point at the time), the average for ten years being 10.3 per thousand.

The grand new suburb of the Seabrook Estate was to cover the mainly undeveloped eastern part of the borough. The plans, however, were largely dependent on whether the

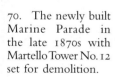

70. The newly built Marine Parade in the late 1870s with Martello Tower No. 12 set for demolition.

71.   During the development of the Marine Parade in the 1870s, the Moyle Tower was planned as a hotel. However this never took place and the building was left as an empty shell for a time before it was completed as a private residence. In 1923 the Holiday Fellowship acquired it as a holiday home.

72.   An advertisement for the West Parade Estate in the 1890s. However, only a few terraces were initially built and the *Marine Hotel* and shops never materialised.

railway was extended from Sandgate Station to Folkestone Harbour and when this failed to take place the scheme foundered. The Seabrook Estate Company, which was formed by SER shareholders, hoped to develop the 500-acre Scene (or Sene) Estate north of Hythe Station but, save for Cliff Road, none of the other roads saw the light of day. The SER had planned to raise the level of the land at Seabrook with spoil from the proposed tunnels at Sandgate and Folkestone Leas, but of course this was not possible while the extension remained

73. This fine pair of oriental shelters became a feature of Marine Parade in June 1896 but disappeared in the 1950s. Beyond the shelters is Beaconsfield Terrace.

74. The *Hotel Imperial* in 1912, which was opened as the *Seabrook Hotel* by the South Eastern Railway on 21 July 1880 at a cost of £30,000.

75. 'Ye Black Cottage' café on Seabrook Road in around 1910, which served snacks and late suppers from 7 a.m. daily right up until 1961.

only on the drawing board. Some members of the Estate Company even threatened to sell their land to the rival London, Chatham and Dover Railway if they succeeded in extending their proposed Alkham Valley line to Hythe (the line was never built). Proposals by the SER to placate the company's shareholders by constructing lines to Seabrook from New Romney and Shorncliffe were non-starters and they turned their attention to killing off the LCDR's Alkham Valley line by opening the Elham Valley Railway from Shorncliffe to Canterbury in 1887-9.

An earlier proposal to develop the Seabrook end of town in 1866 had also failed. The Seabrook Harbour Scheme consisted of a new sea wall on what later became Princes Parade and two breakwaters 600 feet long at Seabrook and Fort Twiss, curved to meet each other at

a breakwater 1,800 feet in length opposite the entrance to the harbour. Passages through the sea wall would lead to docks dug out on the land between the sea and the Hythe-Sandgate road, while the Royal Military Canal would be acquired throughout its length and a railway would connect it to the main line. Unsurprisingly, nothing of this ambitious venture ever saw the light of day.

Eventually, during the 1880s and 1890s, Seabrook was developed with a mixture of middle-class villas and artisan housing by local builder John James Jeal, who had purchased land from the Seabrook Estate. The *Fountain* inn, first mentioned in 1841, was totally rebuilt at a cost of £1,490 in 1887-8 and the *Seaview Hotel*, erected by Jeal at a cost of £1,693, opened a year later. The Seabrook Mission Hall held its first meeting on 3 November 1883 and

76. Pictured in 1909 is the South Eastern & Chatham Railway's parcels and luggage wagon that operated from Hythe station.

was also used as a school, being joined by the opening of Seabrook School in 1897. Work had commenced on building the school on 19 September 1896 thanks to a legacy from the late Mrs Thompson of Seabrook Vale. In 1994 it was enlarged with a new library, classroom and storage room.

Seabrook's development was commented upon in Wilson's *Guide to Sandgate, Shorncliffe & Hythe*:

Seabrooke, previous to 1881, was looked upon as part of Sandgate, but

its development in that year claimed its separation. A number of houses were erected and a few shops and since that year it has been gradually increasing. Its enlargement is entirely due to Mr John James Jeal, who bought a lot of land from the Seabrook Estate Company and commenced building. On May 15th 1883, the foundation stone of some mission buildings for religious worship and a national school was laid by Mrs F.D. Brockman of Beachborough, the services being conducted by Dr Parry, Bishop of Dover.

77. Hythe's eastern suburb of Seabrook, seen in around 1906. Eastcote Villas on the left were erected as part of the late Victorian/early Edwardian development of the area. The Royal Military Canal can also just be seen.

78. An early 1900s view of Seabrook looking east towards Sandgate and Folkestone.

79. The *Fountain Hotel* and Seabrook Road in around 1911 on a postcard published by HB's F&L. This second
version of the pub was designed by Mr Fry and erected in 1888-9 by Mr Brooks at a cost of £1,490.

John James Jeal had come to live in Seabrook in 1881 and, as well as building most of the houses, the mission hall, school and *Seaview Hotel*, he erected the Cheriton Schools and laid the tramway from Hythe to Sandgate. He first entered Hythe Town Council on 1 November 1882 and was mayor in 1902-3 and 1903-4, although he once resigned from the Council in order to fight them on the vexed question of Seabrook's drainage. Mr Jeal was an active member of the community and it was said there were few local institutions with which he was neither directly or indirectly involved. Only hours before his death on 19 June 1920 he had been entertaining David Lloyd George and Field-Marshal Foch at Hythe Golf Course clubhouse.

Another SER plan which never quite reached full fruition was the Hythe-Sandgate horse tramway, known as the 'Four Mile Ride by the Sea'. This was opened by the Folkestone, Sandgate and Hythe Tramways Company in three sections: Sandgate Esplanade to *Seabrook Hotel* via Princes Parade on 18 May 1891; *Seabrook Hotel* to Red Lion Square, Hythe via South Road and Stade Street on 1 June 1892, and Sandgate Esplanade to Sandgate Hill on 1 August 1892. The SER operated the 4ft. 8½in. standard-gauge line from the start and officially took it over on 24 June 1893. Their aim was to electrify the line and extend it into Folkestone, but opposition from Folkestone's aristocratic West End killed the plan and the tramway settled down to become principally a popular summer attraction for visitors. Out of the five vehicles used on the tramway, the open-topped No. 5, dubbed the 'Toastrack', was undoubtedly the most popular, except of course in wet weather! Following the suspension of the

service in the First World War, it was restarted in May 1919 with mules, owing to the shortage of horses. However, their occasional stubborn nature meant they sometimes failed to halt at the required stops or take the tram where it was meant to go! Horses were reinstated, but by now the tram was viewed as a slow, traffic-delaying relic of a bygone age and the final trip took place on 30 September 1921. The line was officially closed in January 1922, when it was one of only two horse tramways left in England (the last, at Morecambe, closed in 1926). The tramway shed at Red Lion Square survives, complete with the fascia 'Folkestone, Hythe & Sandgate Tramways 1894'.

On 12 February 1862 the popular open space known as the Green, where the old twice-yearly medieval fairs were held, was established for 'public recreation with no part of it to be applied for building purposes'. The land had been purchased from the War Department with monies principally donated by Joseph Horton and George Shipdem. The Green was used for circuses, such as the visit of the Worlds Fair on 27 June 1896, which housed a 'Gigantic Circus, Mammoth Hippodrome, Grand Double Menagerie and Museum of the world's greatest freaks and curiosities'. Two years later, Charlie the Elephant, remembering where he had been fed some apples outside a greengrocer's shop, broke free from Sangers Circus in the early hours and proceeded to the shop where he forced the door and helped himself to the stock of fruit and veg! In 1900, Charlie and another elephant had to be shot after breaking out of their quarters at Crystal Palace.

The American Gardens at Saltwood, laid out by Archdeacon Croft, were another visitor attraction. First advertised in 1897, the gardens

80.   The Hythe-Sandgate Horse Tramway pictured in around 1910 at Red Lion Square.

featured fine specimens of rare American and Japanese shrubs, forest trees, conifer, bamboo, rhododendrons and azaleas. On the sea front Mr A.C. Leney opened his grounds at Saltwood Gardens to the public during the summer. Mr Leney donated the 6d. entrance fees to local good causes, including the Royal Victoria Hospital in Folkestone.

The Hythe Venetian Fête on the Royal Military Canal was said to have begun in the 1860s as part of Hythe Cricket Week, yet it was not until the 1890s that it grew into an annual event. It featured a procession of gaily-decorated craft, and the elm trees lining the canal were festooned with fairy lights and Chinese lanterns, presenting a most colourful sight. The Cricket Week itself was held during the second week of August and was the social event of the year. Matches were held against famous teams such as I Zingari, the Band of Brothers (led by Lord Harris, Captain of England 1878-80)

and the Free Foresters. A.P.F. Chapman, captain of Kent and England, was a member of the club between the wars and once hit a six into the canal. An Olde English Fayre was set up during the Cricket Week with sideshows such as shooting saloons and coconut shies. There were also torchlight military tattoos and firework displays. Hythe had its own golf course close to the station, boasting a most splendid 19th hole.

Bordering the canal on its north bank was an attractive area of trees and flowers known as the Grove. The area featured a bandstand, a popular rendezvous for the Hythe Town Military Band, formed in 1880. During the summer of 1896, as well as performing in the Grove, they could be heard on the lawn at the Elms, and on 31 July 1897 led a Grand Military and Vocal Concert held at Moyle Tower. The grounds were especially illuminated for the event and a 1s. admission was charged, yet the

81. A mule-powered tram leaves Princes Parade, Seabrook shortly after the ending of the First World War. The unpredictable mules were used owing to the shortage of horses, huge numbers of which had been killed in the war.

82. A charabanc trip waits to set off from the High Street in around 1912. In the background on the corner with Douglas Avenue is the Hythe branch of the Co-op. The building land advertised for sale was not developed until 1932.

83. Two motor buses in Military Road *c.*1910 touting for custom. In the background is the *Ordnance Arms*, now the site of a petrol station.

84. The American Gardens, Saltwood, laid out by Archdeacon Croft and opened in 1897. The gardens were famous for their rare American and Japanese shrubs and rhododendrons and azaleas.

85.   Looking across its small village green, Saltwood's *Castle Hotel* is seen in the early years of the 20th century. On the left is the premises of Walter Spratt, family grocer and provision merchant.

86.   The staff of Parson's Library pose for one of their own postcards during a picnic outing in around 1912.

87.   The Hythe Town Military Band pose on the cricket ground in all their finery, including an impressive array of medals and a trophy resting on the big bass drum.

event was described as a fiasco when no one turned up! In 1900 the band split into two, with one group forming the Hythe Town Excelsior Band; in 1903 they were reunited.

In addition to the Hythe Town Military Band, there was also the Promenade Band and the Hythe Professional String Band. In 1896 the Imperial Black & White Minstrels spent a season at Hythe. During the morning they appeared as minstrels with burnt cork on their faces, and in the evening wore smart dress. The troupe consisted of five gentlemen and one lady and performed a mixture of comedy, song, mime and magic. The original Hythe Minstrels, the Mohicans, commenced their fifth consecutive season at Hythe that year, sometimes appearing at the Institute.

The Hythe Institute was located opposite the Grove in Prospect Road and was opened in 1892 by Alfred Bull in his converted house. Used as a concert hall, reading room, games room and subscription library by both locals and visitors,

88.   A favourite summer afternoon Edwardian treat was a trip to Gravener's Tea Gardens and Tennis Courts at West Hythe. Mrs Ellen Gravener also ran the Coronation Tea Rooms in the High Street between 1907-21.

89. Opened in 1892 by local builder and benefactor Alfred Bull, the Hythe Institute in Prospect Road contained a concert hall, reading room and subscription library. This postcard shows it in 1913, for in 1968 the building was demolished for road widening.

90. A fancy dress dance for children held at the Hythe Institute in January 1914.

91. The Oddfellows Hall pictured shortly after it was opened in 1903.

no gambling or alcohol was allowed. Grand Evening Concerts were a feature and in August 1897 the bill featured moving pictures, variety artists Valentine Smith and Miss McBride, and Prince Umbetiguasanghanghamo delivering a humorous and instructive description of the various peoples of Tropical Africa (although he attracted only a very small audience and the paper omitted his name through lack of space!) There was also the Walford family of Campanologists Royal (250 bells of 'Hydro-daktulopsychicharmonica'), an oriental string band and William Fannington's 24-inch high marionette dwarfs with living heads. During Hythe Cricket Week the Hythe Institute would hold a variety of events, as would the nearby Oddfellows Hall.

Moving pictures had been shown in both the Institute and Town Hall since 1896, but Hythe's first permanent cinema, the Electric

92. The eastern end of the High Street in around 1913, featuring the *Wilberforce Temperance Hotel*, Coronation Tea Rooms and the Hythe Picture Palace. An arcade of ten shops was built on the site of the Picture Palace in 1928 and in 1933 the hotel and tearooms were demolished to provide a site for Woolworth's and Sainsbury's.

93.   Hythe in the snow, possibly following a heavy fall in March 1909. The Methodist Church can be seen on the left and St Leonard's Church is up on the hill.

94.   A delightful postcard by Parson's Library of children skating on the frozen pond at Saltwood village green in February 1912.

95.   The result of the Easter Storm of 22/23 March 1913 when heavy seas demolished the sea wall and promenade on West Parade causing £10,000 worth of damage. This postcard was produced by the local photographer Charles Aldridge of the Wellington Studio.

Theatre in the High Street, was not opened until 12 April 1911. Designed by A.P. Bowles and erected by Scott Bros, the cinema, which altered its name to the Hythe Picture Palace in May 1912, became renowned for its smart dome-shaped paybox covered in gold leaf. The programmes, featuring all the latest releases, were changed twice weekly and became particularly popular during the First World War when many Canadian soldiers were based in the area. The auditorium could seat up to 450 people, who paid admission prices ranging from 3d. to 1s. However, upon the opening in May 1927 of the Grove Cinema, the Picture Palace was closed and its staff were transferred to the new cinema.

Hythe has also suffered its fair share of dramatic moments. On 1 January 1877 a great storm led to the sea's reclaiming all the land up to the Royal Military Canal by breaking through temporary sea defences. These were in place because workmen were using shingle in the construction of new properties on Marine Parade. Hurricane-force winds fanned the midday high tide and as the water poured down Stade Street many householders had to be rescued from upstairs windows. Ladies Walk and Scanlons bridges were destroyed and Stade Street bridge was badly damaged as the sea returned to its old haunts bordering the High Street.

The sea front took another battering during the evening of 22/23 March 1913, when storm-driven heavy seas scoured away the sea wall and promenade on West Parade, causing £10,000 worth of damage. The seafront properties were badly affected as seawater poured into their basements, flooding rooms and destroying furniture.

Unfortunately these disasters were to pale into insignificance compared with what was to come the following year.

9
Two Wars and a Peace

Hythe returned to war on 4 August 1914 and soon became full of troops once again, principally Canadians based in the camps at Shorncliffe, Otterpool and Sandling that ringed the town. During the night of the Zeppelin raid of 13/14 October 1915, when 71 people were killed around the country, Otterpool Camp was targeted by Zeppelin L14 (LZ46), which dropped four bombs at around 9.15 p.m. Fifteen men of the 8th Howitzer Brigade and 5th Brigade of Canadian Field Infantry lost their lives and another 21 were injured; in addition seven horses were killed. After two HE bombs had been dropped on the racecourse at Westenhanger, *Kapitanleutnant* Alois Bocker directed the airship out to sea at Hythe but, having found his bearings, then came inland again at Littlestone. The line of the coast was then followed as far as Pett, near Hastings, before L14 headed north.

On Friday 25 May 1917 Hythe was targeted by German Gotha bombers during their first daylight raid on England that was to cause such horrific casualties in nearby Folkestone. Sixteen bombs (seven 50kg and nine 12½kg) were dropped on Hythe, causing two fatalities. Three of the bombs failed to explode, two of them dropping through houses in Cobden Road and West Parade, while seven fell on the beach and in gardens and allotments, injuring

96. A view of Reachfields Camp in around 1914, showing the soldiers washing up after dinner. A housing estate now covers the site.

97.   The 69th Field Company Royal Engineers, based at Shorncliffe Camp, on bridge-building exercises on the Royal Military Canal at Seabrook in November 1914. In the background is the *Seaview Hotel*.

one man. Another fell harmlessly on Hythe Golf Course and one exploded above the Metropole Steam Laundry, where splinters penetrated the roof, fortunately without anyone being hurt. The deaths were caused by a bomb that fell in the parish churchyard, killing Daniel Stringer Lyth, and two that burst in the air, shrapnel from one of which fatally injured Amy Parker. The final two bombs fell on rough ground and the Imperial Hotel Golf Course close to the Royal Military Canal.

Surprisingly, the RFC School of Aerial Gunnery at West Hythe was not attacked, and because they were trainees the pilots were

98.   A postcard showing an open-air religious service for soldiers in the fields off South Road, *c.*1914. The pair in the foreground appear to be taking more notice of the photographer than of what the priest is saying!

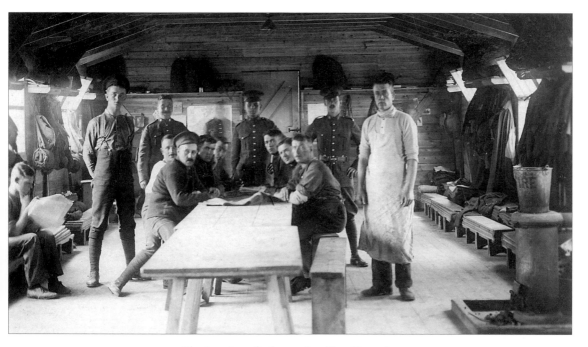

99. The interior of a hut at Sandling Camp in 1915.

unable to scramble any of their planes. This led to some hostility from townsfolk after the raid, who branded the pilots useless and were reported to have thrown bricks at them.

Mr Lyth was verger of St Leonard's Church and a former town sergeant. He was killed by a bomb splinter that ripped into his right thigh while standing at the west door of the church. He had been engaged in conversation with the vicar, Rev. H.D. Dale and his wife inside the church when they heard the explosions outside. On going to investigate a bomb fell in the churchyard shattering tombstones and sending shrapnel in all directions. The vicar was saved from injury by a tin of throat lozenges in his coat pocket that deflected a piece of shrapnel, although his wife was injured in the face. Mrs Parker, of Ormonde Road, was killed by a bomb splinter that entered her left breast when she went outside to call her child indoors. Two

further people, Emily and Jane Nicholls of 12 Albert Road, were injured.

Continuing to hug the coast, the raiders flew eastwards, the northern flank attacking Shorncliffe Camp (where 18 soldiers were killed) and Cheriton (three killed), and the southern flank Sandgate. The planes then converged over Folkestone where 51 bombs were dropped. Seventy-two people, consisting principally of women and children, were killed, with one bomb falling among shoppers in Tontine Street accounting for 61 of them.

During the same year, on 2 April 1917, the Hythe lifeboat *Mayer de Rothschild (III)* was involved in the dramatic rescue of the ketch *Mazeppa* in a strong south-easterly gale, which led to Coxswain Dearman and 2nd Coxswain Wright Griggs being awarded the RNLI Bronze Medal. The *Mazeppa* had entered Hythe Bay for shelter, yet her anchor had begun to drag and she looked likely to be driven ashore. Distress signals fired by the crew were seen and the Hythe lifeboat was launched, but only after a delay in pulling it over the beach during driving rain. Nevertheless, the lifeboat managed to reach the stricken ketch and after casting anchor was able to rescue the crew. Owing to the rough sea, Dearman decided it would be better to cut away the anchor rather than raise it and, rowing through the rough sea, managed to reach the shore safely.

The Mayor of Hythe during the war, William Cobay, raised £554 for the Kent Volunteer Fencibles and the East Kent Regiment, Cinque Ports Battalion F (Hythe) Company, who could be seen practising their skills in the town before marching off to war. In addition, he raised money for other war causes and in January 1918 inaugurated the Hythe Heroes Fund to assist returning wounded troops and families of those who had been killed. In recognition of his splendid wartime service Mr Cobay was made a Freeman of the Borough in 1919.

Two Hythe men, Captain John Francis Vallentin (South Staffordshire Regiment) and Lieutenant Gordon Steele RN, won Victoria Crosses. Captain Vallentin's was presented posthumously after he was killed near Ypres on 7 November 1914. He was leading an attack that eventually captured a strategically important German trench. Lieutenant Steele was honoured with a VC for his part in a torpedo boat attack on the Bolsheviks during the Russian Civil War. In addition, Military Medals were awarded to Lance Corporal Dawkins (London Regiment) and Guardsman

100.   A rare aerial view of the RFC School of Gunnery Airfield at West Hythe in around 1917. The coast road from Dymchurch can be seen snaking in from the right. On its seaward side are the Hythe Ranges and Dymchurch Redoubt.

101. A fund-raising fête held for the war effort by the Red Cross, pictured in September 1916.

102. The civic dignitaries of Hythe march across Prospect Road on their way to unveil the war memorial in the Grove on 16 July 1921.

103.   The war memorial and First World War tank in the Grove, 1923. Hidden behind the memorial can just be seen the field gun that was also presented to the town.

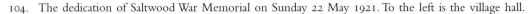

104.   The dedication of Saltwood War Memorial on Sunday 22 May 1921. To the left is the village hall.

105. The south front and terrace of Port Lympne, erected in 1911-13 by Sir Herbert Baker for Sir Philip Sassoon at a cost of £250,000.

Page (Grenadier Guards). A Military Cross was presented to Frederick William Butler, five times mayor in 1909, 1910, 1926, 1930 and 1936, and he was granted the Freedom of the Borough in 1938.

Hythe emerged from the Great War relatively unscathed and on 11 July 1919 received two mementoes of it in the shape of a tank and a field gun (Seabrook also received a field gun). They were presented by Sir William Tritton, President of the War Tank Association, and placed in the Grove, where on 16 July 1921 they were joined by the war memorial. Designed by Gilbert Bays and unveiled by the Lord Warden of the Cinque

Ports, Earl Beauchamp, the surrounding wall of the memorial recorded the 154 Hythe men who fell in the war. A further 63 names were to be added later, recalling those who fell in the Second World War.

The vexed questions of the peacemaking were sometimes solved at the home of the town's MP Sir Philip Sassoon, Port Lympne, built between 1911-13 at a cost of £250,000. The Right Hon. Sir Philip Albert Gustave David Sassoon BT, GBE, CMG, MP was born in 1888 to Sir Edward Albert Sassoon and Alice Caroline, daughter of Baron Gustave de Rothschild. He was educated at Eton and Christ Church, Oxford and in 1912 succeeded

106.   Lympne village slumbers in the afternoon sun, c.1920. The castle can just be seen on the left.

his father as Unionist MP for Hythe. During the war he had held a commission in the Royal East Kent Yeomanry and in December 1915 was appointed Private Secretary to Field Marshal Haig. In 1920 he was chosen as Private Secretary to Lloyd George and had two spells as Under-Secretary for Air in 1924-9 and 1931-7. Sir Philip then became the First Commissioner of Works in Neville Chamberlain's administration, but following an illness he passed away at his Park Lane home on 3 June 1939.

Sir Herbert Baker had designed Port Lympne with a Roman feel in accordance with Sir Philip's wishes. This was accentuated in the splendid entrance hall with its marble columns, stone staircase, fountains, and black and white tiled floor. The drawing room featured an African mural by Jose-Marie Sert that was destroyed in the Second World War, while the dining

room housed an Egyptian-style frieze by Glen Philpott. Other features of the house included an octagonal library and a Moorish patio-courtyard with white stone walls, colonnaded arcades, exotic flowers and orange trees. The 15-acre gardens boasted a large swimming pool, flanked by two smaller pools, all complete with fountains. There was also a great Trojan stairway of 125 steps, originally surmounted by two Roman pavilions that were removed in 1920, and terraced borders of herbaceous plants, figs and vines.

During the 1920s and '30s, the house became well known through Sir Philip's weekend parties with their guest lists of the rich and famous. These included the Prince of Wales (later Edward VIII), the Duke of York (George VI), Winston Churchill, Charlie Chaplin, David Lloyd George, T.E. Lawrence and George Bernard Shaw. In 1933 Rex

107. The people of Seabrook greet the Prince of Wales as he passes through on 27 July 1921 on his way to Port Lympne, the home of Sir Philip Sassoon. The Prince was returning from Folkestone where he had laid the foundation stone for the new nurses' home at the Royal Victoria Hospital.

Whistler was commissioned to paint the renowned Tent Room.

Following Sir Philip's death, Port Lympne passed to his cousin Hannah Gubbay. Eventually, in 1973, Sir John Aspinall acquired the estate at a cost of £400,000 and opened it to the public in 1976 as a wild animal park, with an emphasis on conservation. During his lifetime Mr Aspinall sympathetically restored both house and garden to something akin to their former splendour.

The sylvan and understated charms of Hythe as a seaside resort were at their most popular during the inter-war years and were actively promoted by both the Hythe Chamber of Commerce and the Southern Railway. The

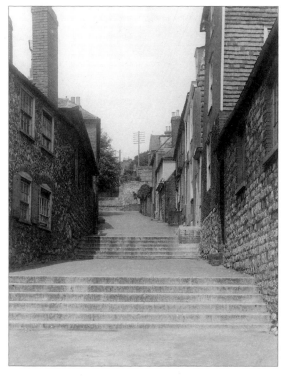

108. The charm of old Hythe in the 1920s, as Church Hill winds up the hillside to the parish church of St Leonard.

109.   The Royal Military Canal on a fine summer's day in the 1920s.

110.   An Arcadian view of the Grove and bandstand on a summer's day in the 1920s with the sun glinting through the trees.

111. A photograph from the 1920s showing a tennis tournament in progress in the grounds of the *Hotel Imperial*.

112. A 1930s view of the Venetian Fête float of Plummer Roddis. Describing themselves as 'Folkestone's leading fashion store', they were particularly keen to advertise their 'undies and millinery'.

113.   Marine Parade in the late 1920s. On the left can be seen the shelter and entrance in the Pavilion Gardens, erected in 1924.

designation *Pride of Kent* was coined in 1924 and a poster produced in the 1930s shows bathers frolicking in front of a fishing or pleasure boat, while in the background on West Parade stands Martello Tower No. 13 following its conversion into a house. The Venetian Fête and Cricket Week remained popular attractions, the latter given a boost by the fact that Hythe Cricket Club's Percy Chapman (who worked as an under-brewer at the Mackeson Brewery) was England cricket captain between 1926-30.

The quiet ambience of Hythe particularly appealed to middle-class couples and families,

114.   The beach in the 1930s, with a row of gaily striped beach huts on the shingle.

such as Leonard and May Sutton, who both worked in a hospital as administrator and matron respectively. The following is an account of their stay in Hythe in 1920:

June 21st – Left Redhill at 10.55 a.m., arrived Hythe 12.20 p.m. [presumably by train]. Lunch at the Temperance Hotel; unpacked in the afternoon and went for a walk along the canal. May found sixpence. Strolled along the seafront after supper.

June 22nd – Shopping in the morning; visited the crypt, St Leonard's Church where the skulls are stacked. A large flying boat alighted on the sea opposite the Imperial Hotel about midday; left again about 2 p.m. Walked to Saltwood village in the afternoon; had tea there, came 'home' and spent the evening on the beach.

June 23rd – 'Carnation Day'. Went to Folkestone by bus; bought a cap, some vases, crested china and something 'in remembrance'. Came home by bus and went on the beach in the evening.

June 24th – Spent a lazy morning on the beach; went on the canal in the afternoon; had tea at Cooper's Gardens, and some fine strawberries. Came back and went on the beach in the evening.

June 25th – Walked to Dymchurch, about five miles; paddled and had a race in the sand. Visited the Old English Church; came home by bus in the evening. Had supper and a walk on the beach.

June 26th – Shopping in the morning; bought stockings, socks and tomatoes. Went on the canal in the afternoon; had tea at Cooper's Gardens. May can steer well now, but can't row for nuts. Came home and went on the beach in the evening.

115. The dining room of the Holiday Fellowship Home at the Moyle Tower, Marine Parade in 1937.

116. A bedroom at Philbeach, a convalescent home for workers on London Transport between 1925-88. The home is now a retirement centre.

June 27th – On the beach all day. Went to St Leonard's Church in the evening (our first evening service together); walked home along the seafront.

June 28th – Went to Dover by bus; splendid view of the sea from the cliffs above Folkestone; went on the pier in the morning and the cliffs in the afternoon. Spent hours looking for the Bleriot Memorial; got back too late to go to the museum (May's fault).

June 29th – Shopping in the morning and on the beach. Went to station after dinner, then a farewell row on the canal; pulled

117. The tea garden of Paddock House, Prospect Road in the 1930s. During the First World War the house had been used as an army hospital.

118. A delightful study of Horn Street in the 1920s with the local children happy to pose for the photographer G. Grantham of Seabrook. On the hill in the distance is the parish church of Cheriton, St Martin's.

up to Cooper's Gardens; had raspberries and cream for tea. May nearly upset the boat on the way home.

June 30th – Last day of a glorious holiday; happy days that we shall always remember. The weather has been kind to us and we feel we have made up for the three years we were parted (my service in India during the Great War). Went on the beach in the morning; came home and packed.

May wrote poetry in our excellent Mrs Chittenden's book. Left Hythe 4 p.m., arrived Redhill 5.20 p.m.

The Holiday Fellowship also found tranquil Hythe to their liking and in 1923 moved into Moyle Tower, a large house on Marine Parade that was erected in 1877-8 for use as a hotel. However, it was left as an unfinished shell for a number of years before being converted into a residence for Frederick Porter. The Fellowship ran nearly forty such Christian holiday centres throughout Britain, with an emphasis on exploring the natural beauty of the surrounding countryside. Their guidebook stressed:

A feature of such holidays is the daily excursion, under competent and informed leadership, enabling places of beauty and historical interest to be visited. Tramping on mountain or moorland, through woodlands, or by the seashore is a popular characteristic of such excursions. The evenings provide a variety of social programmes and dancing in which guests co-operate to provide the entertainment. The tradition of these arrangements is to weld the house party into a group of friends, irrespective of class, creed or colour.

119.   Seabrook Garage was opened by F.J. Harlow, automobile and motorcycle engineer, soon after the end of the First World War.

120.   A quiet afternoon in the courtyard of the Pavilion in the 1930s. Customers had the choice of relaxing in either wicker chairs or deckchairs.

121. The Saltwood Miniature Railway in the 1930s. Three rides around the track cost 6d.

Hythe's invigorating sea air also encouraged convalescent homes to open in the area. The largest was Philbeach, opened by the London Transport Benevolent Fund in 1924-5. For a 1d. contribution each per week to the fund, up to 70 women employees or wives of contributors were able to convalesce at the home following a bout of illness or after an operation, along with their children under eight years of age. The home's provision of extensive gardens, outings, concerts, sports and a cinema proved popular and led to its being extended in 1929 and 1937. From the late 1970s men were also admitted, but falling numbers forced London Transport to close the home in 1988 and it is now a retirement centre.

Hythe's glorious Cinque Port past was invoked in 1923 with the erection of the Shepway Cross on the hill where the old Court of Shepway used to meet. The inscription on the cross records that it was erected 'In memory of the historic deeds of the Cinque Ports, on the ancient site of the Shepway Cross,

122. Hythe RHDR Station in 1930. The writer of the postcard has commented, 'Don't you think this tiny railway is very quaint? When it stops at the station you can put your hand out and touch the platform.'

123.   The entrance to RHDR station in the 1930s, showing Henry Greenly's original building and the adjoining Light Railway Restaurant.

by William Seventh Earl of Beauchamp, KG Lord Warden and Admiral 1923'.

That same year another drinking fountain was presented to Hythe and was sited at the south end of Ladies Walk near the Moyle Tower and Neptune Cottage (now the yacht club). It boasted a bowl at the base for pets and a drinking mug on a chain. An inscription read 'Cherie Avril, ballet dancer for charities' and the

date of presentation. The fountain was removed in the Second World War to be melted down for the war effort. The year 1923 also saw the first concrete sound mirror dish erected on the Roughs above Hythe as part of a proposed acoustic sound defence system developed by Dr W.S. Tucker of the Air Defence Experimental Establishment. A larger 30-foot dish was added in 1929, which still survives (the earlier 20-foot

124.   A view of Mount Street towards the High Street in the 1920-30s. The Grove Cinema, affectionately known as the 'Shack', can be seen on the left.

dish was lost to land slippage in the 1980s), but the system was to be superseded by radar in the 1930s.

May 1924 saw the old Bathing Establishment converted into a restaurant and tea room called the Pavilion. A new shelter was erected on Marine Parade in the same classical style, through which access to the Pavilion could be obtained. A Mrs Farmer later leased the property and a music and dancing licence was granted. Roller skating and whist drives were also popular, but in 1953 the Pavilion was closed and subsequently demolished, the shelter suffering the same fate a few years later.

The well-liked Saltwood Model Railway was also opened in 1924. Operated by Frank Schwab in his back garden, the railway was later run by his son Alexander. Hythe's most popular tourist attraction, however, was opened three years later, the world famous Romney, Hythe & Dymchurch Railway. Captain John Edwards Presgrave Howey and Count Louis Zborowski conceived 'The Smallest Public Railway in the World' in 1924, but the latter was killed in a motor race at Monza in October of that year. Zborowski had lived at Higham Park, Bridge and raced the famous Chitty Chitty Bang Bang, star of the 1968 film of the same name. Howey took on the Count's two locomotives that were under construction and asked their creator, Henry Greenly, to design all aspects of the 15-inch gauge railway, including six further locomotives (initially one-third size replicas of Great Northern Pacifics). The route from New Romney to Hythe was recommended to Howey by the Southern Railway (who had toyed with the idea of building a line) as one that would involve very few earthworks over the flat terrain.

Work began in late 1925 at what became the administrative and engineering hub of the railway, New Romney (before the Statutory Order was issued on 26 May 1926!), and on 5 August 1926 the Duke of York drove a train from Jesson (St Mary's Bay) to New Romney. The eight-mile line was officially opened on 16 July 1927 and was extended a further 5½ miles from New Romney to Dungeness on August Bank Holiday 1928. The partnership between Howey and Greenly was broken up in 1929, however, when Greenly left the railway following a dispute over drawings of the two Canadian-style locomotives (the popular *Winston Churchill* and *Dr Syn*).

The new Grove Cinema was opened on 16 May 1927 to a design by A.E. Palmer. Replacing the Hythe Picture Palace and known affectionately as the 'Shack', it was sited on the corner of Prospect Road and Mount Street. The *Folkestone Herald* published this description of the cinema upon its opening:

Situated in a natural setting opposite the Grove, the exterior of the new building suggests nothing that one usually associates with the appearance of a cinema, but is quite in keeping with its surroundings. The approach paths lined with evergreen shrubs give it a pleasing appearance and the scheme of exterior decoration harmonises with the surroundings. The two sturdy oaks at the corner of Mount Street and Prospect Road have been retained – from the Grove the large hall is almost completely hidden. Inside, everything possible has been provided for the comfort of patrons. A particularly pleasant colour scheme in orange and light blue has been carried out and special lighting effects blend nicely

125.   Locals gather to view the stricken steamer *Maruke* beached off Princes Parade in January 1929.

with the scheme. There is no balcony and the seating capacity is about 650. Central heating has been installed with a very efficient system of ventilation. The floor is of pine wood blocks. It is in short, a very comfortable and well-appointed cinema.

The first talkie was shown on 26 May 1930, and later in the decade London & Provincial Cinemas acquired the cinema.

The year 1930 also saw the delivery of a new lifeboat, the motor-driven *City of Nottingham*, donated by the Nottingham Lifeboat Fund. However, the old *Mayer de Rothschild (III)*, that bowed out with a record of 14 rescues from 14 launches, was involved in a couple of incidents off Hythe during its last full year of operation in 1929. On the morning of 28 January 1929 the 4,000-ton Dutch steamer *Maruke*, laden with 11,000 tons of general cargo, was travelling through the English Channel off Dungeness when she

was hit by the Greek-registered *Halcyon*. Her hull suffered some damage and she began to list, which prompted her mainly Chinese and Malay crew to hoist the distress flags and fire flares. In response, the Dover tugs *Lady Brassey* and *Lady Duncannon* proceeded to Dungeness and took the *Maruke* in tow. Unfortunately, the sea rapidly began to fill the hold of the damaged vessel and it seemed likely she would sink before Dover Harbour was reached. It was therefore decided to beach the *Maruke*, and at around 5p.m. she was run aground 500 yards off shore, opposite the *Hotel Imperial*. The crew decided to stay with their vessel and during the evening her brightly lit presence acted like a beacon to the local population, who came in their hundreds to view the stricken ship.

Any hopes of re-floating the *Maruke* during the Tuesday were completely dashed when a severe gale blew up, resulting in a very rough sea. At high tide the bows of the steamer

126. Hythe lifeboat Coxswain Harry 'Buller' Griggs (front row right) pictured in company with other decorated lifeboatmen when collecting his RNLI Silver Medal in April 1930.

127. Fisherman, lifeboat volunteer and keen Salvation Army member Wright Griggs mending nets on the Fishermen's Beach in the 1920s. The gasworks in Range Road can be seen in the background. Born in 1862, Wright fathered 14 children; he died on 18 September 1931.

became awash with water and the interior was flooded after the sea broke through the ship's hatches. The distress flags were hoisted once again, which prompted the *Lady Brassey* to attend speedily. This time there was no alternative but to take the crew off the stricken ship. They were put aboard the tug and safely landed at Dover. The Hythe lifeboat *Mayer de Rothschild (III)* had also responded to the distress signals, but reached the *Maruke* after the tug, and so found it deserted.

An inspection of the *Maruke* by a special officer of the Salvage Association during the Wednesday found it to be in poor condition. Firepeaks 1 and 2, the stokehold and the amidships accommodation were flooded with water and hatches 1 and 2 had been washed away. The collision damage was found to extend 14 feet below the upper deck of the starboard bow. After a frustrating few days, when bad weather halted all attempts to move the vessel, the tugs finally managed to tow it to Dover

128.   Old fishermen's cottages near West Parade in the 1920s, one of them advertising teas. They were pulled down in the late 1930s.

129.   The western end of the High Street in the 1920s at the junction with Bank Street. The delivery boy for the World's Stores has parked his bicycle against the kerb without fear of its being stolen.

130. A between-the-wars photograph of Red Lion Square with an interesting array of buses and a Sainsbury's delivery van on show. Notice how empty the roads are.

Harbour, where she was repaired and lived to steam another day.

In the same year Coxswain Harry Buller Griggs (who had succeeded Coxswain Dearman in 1919) won the RNLI Silver Medal when the Hythe lifeboat assisted its Dungeness counterpart in rescuing the crew of the barge *Maggie May* on 12 November 1929.

However, some of the brave Hythe boatmen were finding it increasingly difficult to make a living from their main occupation, fishing. By the First World War drift netting as a whole was

131. A 1937 view of Seabrook showing the bus garage erected on part of Sandgate Station which closed in 1931. The remains of the platforms are still noticeable in the picture.

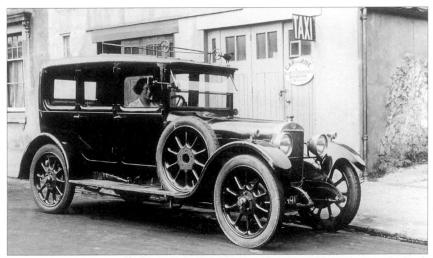

132. Miss Marie West, taxi cab proprietor, pictured in Horn Street opposite the *Fountain Hotel* with one of her first cars. Miss West operated the business from 1926 until 1971.

in serious decline and almost collapsed in the 1920-30s owing to a number of factors. These included a decline in the demand for herring and mackerel, low prices for European imports, and the high price of retail fish leading to less being sold. Hythe's few remaining fishing craft had to contend with dwindling stocks on the outside grounds due to over-fishing up to the six-mile limit by foreign trawlers. Trammelling, an old Cinque Ports method of fishing whereby a series of nets is fixed on the sea bed, has made a comeback in recent years, as have gill nets, so named because fish are caught by the gills behind their heads. Five types of fish that are particularly prized locally are Dover sole, plaice, turbot, cod and dogfish. Mackerel, herring

133. The *Stade Court Hotel*, on the corner of Stade Street and West Parade, pictured around the time of its opening in 1938. A feature of the hotel was Dr Syn's Parlour, a fully licensed restaurant serving lunches, teas and dinners.

134. The bridge over the Royal Military Canal at Seabrook in 1932. The structure was replaced after the Second World War.

and sprats are still caught, as are lobsters, crab, shrimps and whelks.

Another casualty of the inter-war period was the section of railway between Hythe and Sandgate. The Southern Railway, which had taken over the branch on Grouping in 1922, had taken note of ever-falling passenger numbers and closed the line on 31 March 1931. The remainder of the branch from Hythe-Sandling Junction was singled, with the up branch platform at Sandling being taken out of use. Sandgate Station was quickly demolished to make way for a new bus garage and within a few years houses were being built on top of the old railway embankments at Seabrook.

Cinema, however, was thriving in the 1930s and, ten years after the opening of the Grove Cinema, Hythe was to acquire another picture house with the opening by Union Cinemas on 12 June 1937 of the Ritz on the corner of Prospect Road and East Street. This art deco modernist-style cinema, typical of the period ,boasted a plush interior and air conditioning for up to 858 patrons, although a proposed café never materialised. Seat prices ranged from 6d. to 1s., reduced to 10d. at matinee performances. A year after its opening, the Ritz became part of the ABC chain. A popular venue for dancing in Hythe during the 1930s was the Canal Hall.

The late 1930s also saw improvements to the sea front. In 1938 the *Stade Court Hotel* and Four Winds restaurant were opened on West Parade, the Four Winds being a fine example of a 1930s art deco minimalist building. Princes Parade was improved during the same year,

135. Schoolchildren enjoy a ride on the roundabout in the Princes Parade recreation ground at Seabrook in 1928.

1928 and a new lifeboat *Viscountess Wakefield* (costing £6,000) and lifeboat house (£4,000) in 1936. A rose-covered pergola walk on the Recreation Ground was named after him, and he was made an Honorary Freeman of the Borough. Following the death of Lord and Lady Wakefield in 1941 and 1950 respectively (they were laid to rest in Spring Lane Cemetery, Seabrook), the Wakefield Trust, which is still active today, was set up to benefit the poorer people of the town. On 6 May 1957 a special 'Wakefield Day' was held to honour the town's great benefactor. Among those who attended were the Lord Mayor of London and the mayors of the Cinque Ports and their limbs.

Another generous benefactor was Dr Randall Davis, who bequeathed his house Oaklands to Hythe Corporation providing part of it was used as a local history museum. This was duly carried out, the house being converted into offices, a library and local history room, while the grounds were laid out as a park, complete with a bandstand.

Coxswain Griggs won further distinction in 1937 when he received an RNLI Vellum Certificate for rescuing the three crew of the Folkestone motor vessel *Josephine II* on the night of 13 December 1936. Unfortunately, his good name was tarnished when it was alleged that he refused to allow the Hythe lifeboat to take part in the Dunkirk rescue of 1940 and tried to entice the Walmer and Dungeness crews to do the same. His prediction that the *Viscountess Wakefield* was not suitable to run on to the beach at Dunkirk was proved right when the vessel suffered serious damage and was lost (with a record of nine rescues from 17 launches), although the other Kent

thanks largely to the generosity of Lord Charles Wakefield, a generous benefactor to Hythe, who was head of the Wakefield Oil Company. Lord Wakefield was born in London in 1859 and first came to Hythe in 1912. Liking the town, he acquired a cottage in Blackhouse Hill before building his own mansion, The Links. (The house was later renamed Bassett House and was used as a hospital in the Second World War.) In 1915 he was elected Lord Mayor of London and 15 years later in 1930 was honoured by his adopted town as Baron Wakefield of Hythe, which was upgraded to Viscount four years later. Amongst his other generous acts for the town were the recasting of three bells of St Leonard's Church in

136. The aftermath of the bomb that devastated the High Street on 4 October 1940. The completely destroyed Arcade was situated where the gap is in the foreground. On the left is the Congregational Church.

lifeboats did manage the feat. However, Buller continued to rescue people stranded in the Channel, including a downed German pilot, using his own boat.

At the onset of the Second World War in 1939 the Small Arms School took over responsibility for the defences in the area. A sea mine and boom defence system was installed in Hythe Bay and a minefield laid on the seaward side of Hythe Gasworks. The beach was defended with a gantry of scaffold poles with attached mines and six-inch gun emplacements were located on the Promenade. Ladies Walk Bridge was demolished as a defensive measure, and others were disabled. The Royal Military Canal was enmeshed in barbed wire. One of the RHDR engines, *Hercules*, was converted into an armoured train using guns salvaged from crashed aircraft.

As the threat of invasion loomed, the Small Arms School was largely exiled to Bisley. Hythe became a prohibited zone and could be entered only with a valid resident's pass; local children were evacuated to safe areas. The district south of the Royal Military Canal was cleared and declared strictly out of bounds.

Due possibly to its closeness to Lympne Airfield (which suffered a number of heavy attacks), Hythe was subject to 19 air raids and two bouts of shelling, and 11 doodlebugs fell around the town. Twenty civilians were killed, three of them by a bomb that fell on the Arcade in the High Street on 4 October 1940. The following year, on 24 March 1941, three members of the Wonfor family were killed at 49 Tanners Hill Gardens. In 1942, on 10 May, two people died when a bomb fell at the back of Trice's refreshment rooms and three others perished when a bomb exploded in the air above Prospect Road/Bank Street on 21 August. The worst incident of all took place on 15 August 1944 when a doodlebug flattened Nos 1–5 Earlsfield Road claiming five lives.

A further tragedy occurred on 24 February 1941 when ten men of the 2/7 Battalion the Queens Royal Regiment were fatally wounded whilst crossing a minefield near Hythe. Two days later three other soldiers were killed by a bomb that landed on the ranges.

By 1944 Hythe was being described by a Mr H. Wallett as a 'quiet, undisturbed, little town, where lots of the houses had been closed down'.

10

Forward to the New Century

The years since the Second World War have seen Hythe develop as an attractive residential town, with a sprinkling of light industry to combat the decline in tourism and the loss of old established employers such as the Mackeson Brewery and the Small Arms School. The surviving buildings of the erstwhile Cinque Port and beyond were overseen by the Hythe Citizens Union (from 1965 the Hythe Civic Society) who were formed in 1945 to draw up a list of buildings of historical and architectural interest they felt were worth reconditioning. One of their early successes was the preservation of the old St Bartholomew's Hospital (Centuries), which was converted into flats.

Saltwood Castle had long been in private hands and was finally restored between 1934-49 by Lady Conway of Allington, who engaged architect Sir Philip Tilden. He added a new wing in the Gothic revivalist style on the north side of the gatehouse to blend with the Tudor wing on the south side. The castle then passed into the hands of Lord (Kenneth) Clark, who in 1970 handed it over to his colourful MP son Alan. Until recent times the grounds, battlements, armoury and undercroft were open to the public.

137. Hythe Station pictured on 13 October 1951, six weeks before the line to Sandling Junction was closed on Saturday 1 December 1951. Nothing remains of this scene now, although the stationmaster's house survives in Cliff Road.

138. The Grove Dance Band, led by Fred Harrison, pictured in 1949.

Lympne Castle had become a farmhouse and in the early 18th century was leased to William Glanville Evelyn. Sometime later it was taken over by the Bridger family. Upon the death of Archbishop Croft in 1860 the castle passed out of the hands of the Archdeaconry for the first time in nearly 800 years, when sold to a Major Lawes of Dover. He decided not to live there but leased the castle and farm to a Mr Stonham. The outer buildings and surrounding wall fell into ruin and the

Great Hall was converted into a two-storey house with partitioned rooms. However, the partitions were removed during the restoration implemented by the new owner, a Mr Tennant, and carried out by Sir Robert Lorimer in 1905, who also added another wing. Mr Tennant was the brother-in-law of Margot, Lady Asquith, the first woman MP, and while she was staying at the castle a group of suffragettes climbed the ramparts to stage a demonstration! Harry Beecham was owner between 1918-47 and

139. The enduring appeal of the RHDR for both young and old alike is illustrated in this photograph of *Winston Churchill* at Hythe in the late 1990s.

then during Harry Margary's time the castle housed a fine collection of reproduction maps and playing cards, along with toys and dolls from Pollock's Toy Museum. The building is now used for private functions such as wedding receptions.

Westenhanger Castle, which since the 18th century had become a romantic, overgrown ruin, was acquired in 1996 by the Forge family and a programme of repair was commenced with assistance from English Heritage. Open days and guided tours have recently been held at the castle. Nearby are two historic barns dating from 1525-1600 with three-inch thick walls of Kentish ragstone.

The need for new council and private housing after the war was paramount, development having commenced in the 1930s. For example, following the closure in 1931 of the Hythe-Sandgate section of the railway, 12 acres of land adjoining Horn Street in

Seabrook was auctioned on 26 October 1933. The first three houses in Naildown Road, on what became known as the Naildown Estate, namely 'South Winds', 'Seabrook Mount' and 'Coastlands', were built in 1936 and Nos 1-8 followed a year later. Council housing was also developed in the area and completed in the post-war years. Other council estates were established at Wakefield Way, Cinque Ports Avenue, the former Small Arms School and Reachfields (replacing the tin town army houses). Private housing developments included Burmarsh Road, Turnpike Close (on Turnpike Camp), London Road, Sene Park and Pennypot.

A guide in the 1950s described Hythe as:

an ideally attractive spot for a holiday, if you are seeking a perfect combination of lovely Kentish countryside and the fresh invigoration of the sparkling sea. For the young, the generous choice of recreational facilities, and, for the not so young, we

140. The miniature railway that was once a feature of the Willow Tree Farm caravan park at West Hythe.

assure the opportunity of indulging in those lazy 'holiday' extravagances which are a luxury in our working life, but which provide a longing in our hearts and which forever remain in our memories.

A romantic vision, perhaps, yet Hythe had its share of supporters who returned to the town year after year. In recent times, in line with the national trend, it was more often for a day trip or short break, rather than a one- or two-week holiday.

The visitors also came increasingly by car, leading to the closure of the railway to Hythe on 1 December 1951. Sandling (now shorn of its Junction title) remains open and is considered the station for Hythe, notwithstanding the good two-mile walk to reach the town! The old 'down' branch platform survives at Sandling, as does the Hythe stationmaster's house, a couple of tunnels and an over-bridge at Horn Street, Seabrook.

The attractions for both locals and visitors have come and gone since the 1950s. A popular feature during the 1950s/60s was the Hythe Summer Theatre in the Institute, a repertory theatre performing over eight weeks. Opposite, in the now demolished Grove Bandstand, were performances by the Nicolson Pipe Band. The Grove Cinema closed its doors for the last time on 1 March 1958 after the presentation of *Man of a 1000 Faces* starring James Cagney. Incredibly, three of the four staff at the cinema at the time had transferred there from the Hythe Picture Palace back in 1927! The building became a car showroom for Southern Autos, whose premises stretched through to the High Street,

141. An aerial view of Lympne Airfield (latterly known as Ashford Airport) in the 1950s. Commercial flights were available to Beauvais and Calais. An industrial estate now covers part of the site.

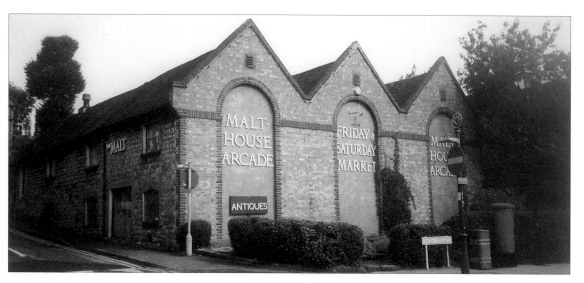

142. The old Malthouse of the Mackeson Brewery, now in use as an antiques market open on Fridays and Saturdays.

but was demolished in the late 1960s for road widening.

Hythe's one remaining cinema, the Ritz, managed to hang on until 7 August 1984. In 1953 it had passed into the hands of London & Provincial Cinemas Ltd, and then in 1966 of Mecca, who used it solely as a bingo hall for the next five years, following which a cinema seating 276 was inserted in the circle. Classic acquired the lease in 1982, but poor attendances led to closure two years later. A block of flats named Blythe Court now stands on the site. For just two years, from 1970-2, a small cinema called the Embassy, seating 100, was housed in a hall behind the Light Railway Café adjoining the RHDR station.

The RHDR itself remains a popular visitor attraction, and rightly so, with its superb fleet of 11 steam and two diesel engines. Yet for a time it too was under threat of closure. The end of the Second World War had found the railway in a poor state, and although the Hythe-New Romney section was reopened on 1 March

1946 the remainder of the line to Dungeness was restored to single track only, later that year. Laurel and Hardy officiated at the reopening on 21 March 1947, and ten years later, on 30 March 1957, the Queen, Duke of Edinburgh, Prince Charles and Princess Anne rode between Hythe and New Romney. Captain Howey died at the age of 76 on 8 September 1963 and the railway entered an uncertain period that saw closure threatened in 1971-2. Fortunately it was rescued by a holding company, led by W.H. McAlpine, which purchased the railway on 14 February 1972. The years since have seen the RHDR built up into one of the major tourist attractions of the south east, popular with young and old alike.

Hythe RHDR station was constructed along with the rest of the railway by Henry Greenly. He placed it in an attractive setting close to the Royal Military Canal at Scanlons Bridge. A new booking hall was added to the station in 1974 and Greenly's two bus shelters that stood outside the station have gone. The

143. Properties along Rampart Road demolished for road widening in the late 1960s. They include Dickie Trice's café, centre right. The photograph was taken by Folkestone historian Eamonn Rooney.

overall roof and four platforms remain, however, as does the signal box, gantry and turntable. Hythe once had two short-lived halts on the railway at Prince of Wales Bridge (1927-8) and Botolph's Bridge (1927-39). For a period of time the people of Hythe could also take to the air locally when up to 18 return flights were available from Lympne Airport to Beauvais (1 hour) and Paris (3 hours).

On the sea front, the Pavilion and oriental shelters disappeared in the 1950s, and in the 1970s the Moyle Tower holiday home was closed. The building was used to house 300 Vietnamese refugees between November 1979 and April 1981 before it was demolished to make way for a block of flats named Moyle Court. The adjoining plot was used to erect a boathouse/clubhouse for the Hythe & Saltwood Sailing Club, which had been formed in 1960 as the Saltwood Sailing Club.

On the Fishermen's Beach, Wright (Sonny) Griggs operated an inshore rescue boat scheme for the RNLI until 1974, using his fishing boats *Our Boys* (FE102) and *Molly Rose* (FE119). Both the old and new lifeboat stations still stand on the beach, where the vessels of the Griggs, Blackman and other Hythe fishing families have been a feature for many years. In addition the Griggs family still runs a fresh fish shop adjoining the beach and the Blackmans have a shop in the High Street.

The number of hotels and guest houses in the town has, not surprisingly, declined in recent years. However, Hythe is fortunate that both

144. A Jack Adams photograph of St Saviour's Hospital, shortly after opening in 1964. Originally part of the Convent of Presentation, the private hospital was acquired by BUPA in June 1989.

the *Imperial* and *Stade Court* hotels remain open (until recently in the hands of W.J. Marston who had acquired the *Imperial* in 1946) and continue to attract residential visitors to the area.

The year 1968 proved to be a difficult one for Hythe as two long-established employers pulled out of the town. Whitbread announced that brewing at the old Mackeson's site was to cease, and five years later the distribution centre was also closed. The majority of the brewery

was subsequently demolished to make way for sheltered housing in 1983, but both the old brewery offices (Elm House) at 1–3 High Street (now flats) and the malthouse (now an antiques centre) still remain.

The old School of Musketry also announced in 1968 that they were leaving Hythe. The continued development of more efficient firearms resulted in a change of name in 1919 to the Small Arms Wing, with a further change

145. The swimming pool in South Road, opened in 1975.

146. Oaklands Bandstand, with the library and museum beyond, in 2003.

to the Small Arms Wing of Hythe School of Infantry occurring in 1947. In 1953, upon its centenary in the town, the school was honoured with the Freedom of the Borough and in return donated the Mayoral Chair, made of oak from a Martello Tower on Hythe Ranges. In December 1968 the school was transferred to the School of Infantry at Warminster, and the buildings were largely demolished for residential and industrial development, although the Commandant's House remains. Between 1853 and 1968 more than 88,000 officers and non-commissioned officers of the British and Commonwealth armies were trained in weapons and marksmanship at the Hythe school, and the term 'Hythe Trained' became synonymous with military excellence.

The Hythe Ranges, on the other hand, in spite of a closure scare in 1969, remain in use. In 1971-2 a mock-up street complete with dummies was erected to provide pre-operational training in counter-insurgency and urban street fighting, then on the increase in Northern Ireland. Two years later, in 1974, the ranges were placed under the Cinque Ports training area and are used by troops from all over NATO.

147. The Hythe Venetian Fête in the 1980s.

148. A poster advertising the 2003 Hythe Venetian Fête. The event is held in odd-numbered years, with the Hythe Festival taking place in the even-numbered years.

In a bid to attract new businesses, industrial estates were created at Pennypot, Range Road and the former refuse site in Dymchurch Road. Large employers such as Portex and Seeboard set up in Hythe and helped ease the loss of the old, established employers. The large supermarkets, though, were resisted for many years until the 1990s saw a branch of Somerfield (now Waitrose) open on the site of the former Conservative Club and health clinic in Prospect Road. This road had been widened in the 1970s to carry the ever-increasing vehicle traffic through the town, which necessitated the closure of the Hythe Institute and its demolition in December 1968. The compensation received

from the Ministry of Transport was used to set up a trust fund, which continues to help worthy causes.

New amenities gained in the past 50 years include a modern library (adjoining the old one in Oaklands) in 1962, which also houses a small museum and local history room. Two years later the private St Saviour's Hospital was opened as part of the Convent of the Presentation and in June 1989 became part of the BUPA organisation. A much-welcomed indoor swimming pool was opened in South Road in 1975. The historic central area of Hythe was designated a conservation area on 14 November 1969, and this was extended on 24 August 1992 to include the area around the canal.

In 1974 Hythe was placed under Shepway District Council, although Hythe Town Council and the mayor remained in place with limited powers. In the late 1980s/early 1990s the attention of the town was directed towards the controversial Port Hythe Marina scheme at Princes Parade, Seabrook, with its proposed 600-berth marina, 405 houses, 193 flats, hotels, restaurant, shops and pubs. Opinions on the plan were divided, with planned alterations to the Royal Military Canal a real concern, but in 1995 it was announced that the scheme had been abandoned.

One course of action universally welcomed was the improvements in 2001-2 to the Royal Military Canal, now scheduled as the third most important linear monument in the country after Hadrian's Wall and Offa's Dyke; the section between Seabrook and West Hythe received a £2.5 million facelift with the assistance of a lottery grant from the Heritage Lottery Fund. Paths alongside the canal were upgraded and colourful information boards provided. The

Seabrook end was equipped with a new car park and play area. Sea defences were improved during the 1990s with the building of rock groynes at Twiss Road and Battery Point, Seabrook to impede the eastward flow of shingle.

Hythe remains a quintessential English town, still a lovely place to visit and live in. A satirical book published in 2003 listed it as the fourth worst town in Britain because it was so 'boring', yet it is because of its quiet charm that Hythe appeals so much to both residents and visitors. Few other towns could offer the choice of spending a warm summer's day strolling along the breezy sea front with its view of the fishing boats and Martello Towers or boating along the tree-lined still waters of the Royal Military Canal, also a popular spot for a few hours of contemplative fishing. The picturesque High Street is a fascinating mix of buildings ancient and modern and houses an equally arresting collection of individual shops. From the High Street, narrow alleys and lanes wind up the hillside to the majestic parish church of St Leonard and its macabre collection of skulls in the crypt.

At Oaklands the Hythe Town Concert Band still performs in the bandstand during the summer months. They have won an impressive list of competitions and medals over the years and played every year for the Queen Mother when she visited Walmer Castle in her capacity as Lord Warden of the Cinque Ports. William Fielder enjoyed playing in the band so much that he was the trombonist for an incredible 62 years (1912-74). The Hythe Venetian Fête remains popular and is now held biannually in odd-numbered years. The mayors of the Cinque Ports head the flotilla of multi-coloured floats, whose theme is kept a closely guarded secret. During even-numbered years the Hythe Festival is held over ten days featuring the Miss Hythe Festival, pop concerts, old time music hall, displays, sports and dog and flower shows. The town can also boast active football, cricket, bowls and tennis clubs.

In 2003 the population of Hythe stood at 14,700, consisting of 2,500 people in the 0-15 age bracket, 7,400 aged between 16 and 59 and 4,700 over-60s.

Bibliography

❧❧

Adamson, R.G., *Hythe: The Holiday Fellowship* (c.1950)

Barker, Jack F., *The Saxon Origins of St Leonard's Church, Hythe* (1984)

Brentnall, Margaret, *The Cinque Ports and Romney Marsh* (1980)

Brooke, Jocelyn, *The Goose Cathedral* (1950)

Carpenter, Edward, *Wrecks and Rescues off the Romney Marsh Coast* (1985)

Clements, W.H., *Towers of Strength: Martello Towers Worldwide* (1999)

Cobbett, William, *Rural Rides* (1830)

Coles Finch, William, *Watermills and Windmills* (1933)

Dale, Rev. H.D., *The Ancient Town of Hythe and St Leonard's Church, Kent* (1931)

Dale, Rev. H.D. and Major O.G. Villiers, *Saltwood Parish Church* (1962)

Davies, W.J.K., *The Romney, Hythe & Dymchurch Railway* (1975)

Easdown, Martin, *A Glint in the Sky* (2004)

Easdown, Martin, *Cries from a Deep Blue Sea* (2004)

Easdown, Martin and Linda Sage, *Hythe in old picture postcards* (2002)

Easdown, Martin and Linda Sage, *Rain, Wreck & Ruin* (1997)

Folkestone Chronicle (various issues)

Folkestone Express (various issues)

Folkestone Gazette (various issues)

Folkestone Herald (various issues)

Folkestone News (various issues)

Forbes, Duncan, *Hythe Haven* (1992)

Griffiths, Pat, *Historical Guide to the Romney, Hythe & Dymchurch Railway* (1976)

Griffiths, Pat, *The History of Port Lympne Mansion and Gardens* (n/d)

Guy, John, *Kent Castles* (1980)

Hart, Brian, *The Hythe & Sandgate Railway* (1987)

Hasted, Edward, *History and Topographical Survey of the County of Kent* (1797-1801)

Hern, Anthony, *The Seaside Holiday* (1967)

Homan, Roger, *The Victorian Churches of Kent* (1984)

Hufton, Geoffrey and Elaine Bird, *Scarecrows Legion: Smuggling in Kent and Sussex* (1983)

Hutchinson, Geoff, *Martello Towers: A Brief History* (1994)

Hutchinson, Geoff, *The Royal Military Canal: A Brief History* (1995)

Hythe Civic Society, *Our Time in Hythe 1945-1995* (1995)

The Hythe Collection of Benjamin Horton held at the East Kent Archives

Hythe Museum, *The Hythe Moot Horn and its History* (1960)

Hythe Reporter (various issues)

Hythe Town Archives assembly books, jurats accounts and other documents

Hythe Town Guides (various years)

Igglesden, Charles, *A Saunter through Kent with Pen and Pencil Vol XXIV* (1930)

Jessup, R.F. & F.W., *The Cinque Ports* (1952)

Kelly's Directory of Folkestone, Sandgate and Hythe (various years)

Kentish Express (various issues)

Klopper, Harry, *To the Fire Committed: The History of Fire Fighting in Kent* (1984)

Maber, Dougie, *The History of the Hythe Ranges* (1998)

Maber, Dougie, *The Hope Inn, Stade Street, Hythe* (1994)

Mackie, S.J., *Folkestone and its Neighbourhood* (1883)

Manning-Sanders, Ruth, *Seaside England* (1951)

Martin, F.H., *Lionel Lukin, 18th Century Life-Boat Inventor* (1982)

Melville, Joy and Angela Lewis-Johnson, *Hythe* (1995)

Melville, Joy and Angela Lewis-Johnson, *Hythe: The Second Selection* (2002)

Miller, G. Anderson, *Noble Martyrs of Kent* (c.1935)

Mothersole, Jessie, *The Saxon Shore* (1924)

Parson's Directory of Folkestone and District (various years)

Philp, Brian, *Romney Marsh and the Roman Fort at Lympne* (1982)

Pike's Folkestone, Hythe and Sandgate Directory (various years)

Pimlott, J.A.R., *The Englishmen's Holiday: A Social History* (1947)

Rainbird, G.M., *Inns of Kent* (1949)

Rayner, Denise, *Fire, Flood & Sudden Death in Old Hythe* (1996)

Rayner, Denise, *The Town Hall of Hythe* (1993)

Roche, Michael, *The Austin Friars in Hythe 1891-1991* (1991)

Scarf, Hilda, *Memories of Hythe in World War II* (1999)

Segar, Rufus, *Remember Hythe: The High Street 1902-1992* (1992)

Snell, J.B., *One Man's Railway* (1983)

Spencer, Diana, *Hythe Police Station 1913-1996* (1999)

Stafford, Felicity and Nigel Yates, *The Later Kentish Seaside* (1985)

Steel, E.A. and E.H. Steel, *The Miniature World of Henry Greenly* (1973)

Sutcliffe, Sheila, *Martello Towers* (1972)

Tapsell, Martin, *Memories of Kent Cinemas* (1987)

Vine, P.A.L., *The Royal Military Canal* (1972)

Walton, John K., *The English Seaside Resort: A Social History 1750-1914* (1983)

Walvin, James, *Beside the Seaside* (1978)

Waugh, Mary, *Smuggling in Kent & Sussex 1700-1840* (1994)

West, Jenny, *The Windmills of Kent* (1979)

Whitney, Charles, *Bygone Hythe* (1989)

Whyman, John, *The Early Kentish Seaside 1736-1840* (1985)

Wilks, G.S., *The Barons of the Cinque Ports* (1892)

Winnifrith, John, *The Royal Military Canal: A History & Guide* (1988)

Wolfe, C.S., *Historical Guide to the Romney, Hythe & Dymchurch Railway* (1976)

Wrottesley, Capt., *A Report on the Royal Military Canal, Hythe* (1857)

Young, Maurice, *The Last Days of Hythe Harbour* (2000)

Index

❧❦

References which relate to illustrations only are given in **bold**